Lebanese Cooking

Dawn, Elaine & Selwa Anthony

PERIPLUS EDITIONS
Singapore • Hong Kong • Indonesia

First published in the United States in 2006 by Periplus Editions (HK) Ltd.,
with editorial offices at at 364 Innovation Drive, North Clarendon, Vermont 05759 USA and
61 Tai Seng Avenue, #02-12, Singapore 534167

Text, photography and design © 2005 Lansdowne Publishing Pty. Ltd.

ISBN 978-0-7946-5024-7

DISTRIBUTED BY

USA
Tuttle Publishing
364 Innovation Drive, North Clarendon, VT 05759-9436
Tel: 1 (802) 773-8930 Fax: 1 (802) 773-6993
info@tuttlepublishing.com
www.tuttlepublishing.com

Japan
Tuttle Publishing
Yaekari Building, 3rd Floor, 5-4-12 Osaki,
Shinagawa-ku, Tokyo 141 0032
Tel: (81) 03 5437-0171 Fax: (81) 03 5437-0755
tuttle-sales@gol.com

Asia Pacific
Berkeley Books (Pte) Ltd
61 Tai Seng Avenue, #02-12, Singapore 534167
Tel: (65) 6280-1330 Fax: (65) 6280-6290
inquiries@periplus.com.sg
www.periplus.com

Text: Dawn, Elaine & Selwa Anthony
Photographer/Stylist: Vicki Liley
Photographer pages 19, 36, 99, 108: Alan Benson/Stylists: Marie-Helene Clauzon, Jane Hann
Photographer pages 57, 115: Andrew Elton/Stylist: Stephanie Souvlis
Designer: Bettina Hodgson
With thanks to (in Australia): Orion Continental Foods, Willoughby, and Frou Frou, Lilyfield

Set in Univers 55 on QuarkXPress

Dedicated to the expert—our mother

Printed in Singapore
12 11 10 09   9 8 7 6 5 4 3 2

contents

introduction

Lebanese cuisine has evolved from a background of Arab culture in a country which has been the trading link between East and West for thousands of years. It is a country which produces ample good, natural food and where people enjoy practising the grace of Arab hospitality. This hospitality requires an abundant table to be set at all times and necessitates a variety of food always being on hand to offer the unexpected guest.

Lebanese cuisine will delight the gourmet, for it is produced by a people who love good food, and satisfy the health enthusiast, because much use is made of grain, cheese, yoghurt, and fresh and dried fruits and vegetables. Even the vegetarian can find many tasty dishes within its scope—meat-free (vegetarian) recipes are marked with the symbol **V** for easy identification, and those that are both meat-free and dairy-free (Lenten) also carry the symbol **L**.

All Lebanese recipes are extremely economical. With imaginative use of herbs, spices, grain and vegetables, meat goes a long way and even the simplest ingredients produce a tasty meal.

Lebanese cooking has been enjoyed for many years by travellers visiting the country, but only recently have Lebanese restaurants been established in any great number in Western countries. This food is now becoming very popular and a curiosity has been aroused about its origin.

To satisfy this curiosity we have included a little of the country's background and a description of the customs and manner of eating. We hope that this will help you to enjoy a truly Lebanese meal.

The recipes in this book have been handed down from mother to daughter for generations. We invite you to try them and wish you Suhtain, which means "enjoy this food in good health".

Dawn, Elaine and Selwa Anthony

A brief guide to Lebanon

Lebanon—the biblical land of the "Song of Songs" and the homeland of the ancient Phoenicians—is one of the smallest and most fascinating countries in the world. Into its small area is packed a wealth of natural beauty and enormous human, historical and archaeological interest.

Measuring only 130 miles (210 km) in length and 46 miles (75 km) in width, it has a population of three million and is situated along the east coast of the Mediterranean between Syria and Israel. Its tiny coastline is dotted with the ancient ports of Tyre, Sidon, Byblos, Tripoli and Beirut.

One third of the total landmass is made up of mountains, which ascend suddenly in places to a height of 8000 feet (2450 metres) and are divided from north to south by the lush Bekaa Valley. On the steep mountain slopes, terraced villages perch precariously amid countless mountain springs and waterfalls.

The sheer sudden height of the mountains becomes obvious when you realise that it is possible, at certain times of the year, to swim in the warm Mediterranean waters at the foot of the mountains and one hour later, after motoring to the top, ski down the snowy slopes.

The Lebanese landscape varies from barren, rocky terrain to fertile valleys and plains. Much of the countryside is covered in cypress, willow, poplar, oak and pine trees, and in places the remains of famous cedar forests are still evident. There are many olive groves and banana plantations, and countless thriving orchards which produce an abundance of citrus fruits, apricots, peaches, figs and pomegranates.

From December through to the northern spring, wildflowers of every colour begin to bloom. Among these are narcissus, iris, crocus, anemone, hibiscus, tulips and cyclamen. In the mountains flowers seem to grow everywhere, even in the stone walls of ancient ruins.

This picturesque country has been called the "Land of the Poets". For thousands of years it has inspired men to sing its praises, among them the great Lebanese poet and philosopher, Khalil Gibran.

Today Lebanon is a country of contrasts and diversities. Beirut, the capital, is a sophisticated city bursting with luxury products, firstclass hotels, elegant women and fast cars. It has also, regrettably, been the scene of complex political conflicts.

These trappings of the modern world stand alongside old souks (marketplaces) and ancient ruins. In the villages people cling to old traditions. They live in simple, stone dwellings and retain a spontaneous outlook on life.

Everywhere you go, you come in contact with the past. Ancient ruins blending into the landscape form a typical characteristic of the country. Archaeological discoveries include Babylonian, Egyptian, Roman, Greek, Byzantine and Arab constructions. Many Roman temples have been transformed into mosques or Byzantine churches and numerous village houses have been built with the debris of ancient monuments.

In the vast complex of the Roman ruins at Baalbeck are the temple of Bacchus, built around 150 AD and much larger than the Parthenon in Greece, and the temple of Heliopolitan Jupiter, the largest and most sumptuous in Roman antiquity. In ancient times this area was called the "granary of the Roman Empire".

The country is also dotted with churches, mosques, convents and monasteries. In the Christian sections, statues to the Virgin and lamp-lit altars are seen along the roadside. The Lebanese are basically very religious, either Christian, Moslem or Druze. Even those who profess atheism adhere to religious customs.

They are also highly educated. As well as many religious schools there are more than 1000 state schools and four universities.

Their heritage is one of academic, trade and cultural achievement. Commencing 3000 years ago with the Phoenicians, the Lebanese were the merchant traders of the ancient world. The phonetic alphabet was developed here, and Phoenician travellers were the first to use the Polar Star for navigation. An interesting note is the flourishing trade they set up in a rare purple dye extracted from shellfish, which became known as "Tyrian Purple". Only wealthy and famous people were permitted to wear this colour, so it became the status symbol of the day. Even now we hear the cliché "born to the purple".

The Arabs left the deepest mark on Lebanese culture and from them the Lebanese took their language. Other early influences came from the Crusaders and the Turks. Modern Western influence arrived when Lebanon became a French Protectorate early in the twentieth century. French and American schools and universities were subsequently established, and today both French and English are spoken widely throughout the country.

The average Lebanese is extremely individualistic. Lebanese people like to "show off'" but have a great sense of dignity and honour. They are always willing to be of assistance and are extremely hospitable. From their Phoenician ancestors they have inherited an aptitude for business dealings and a fondness for travel. These two characteristics could help to account for the fact that the Lebanese are migratory people. It is estimated that there are as many Lebanese settlers abroad as those living in Lebanon. Areas of emigration include the United States, Canada, South America and Australia.

But whether at home or abroad, the Lebanese remain intensely proud of their culture and heritage.

The Lebanese cuisine

It is with food that the Lebanese express their generosity and hospitality. The most casual caller is immediately offered a cup of coffee and even the unexpected visitor is pressed to stay on for an ample meal, which generally consists of a variety of dishes and can always be produced at extremely short notice.

The secret to mastering Lebanese cuisine lies in the preparation and organisation of the menu and in the fact that Lebanese dishes store and reheat well.

The Lebanese cook always prepares several dishes in advance and stores the basic mixtures so that they can be combined with other food items to quickly make a full meal. Every household has a constant stock of pickles, olives, cheese, yoghurt, nuts, grain, herbs and spices.

Nearly every part of the raw product is utilised. In fact there is so little wastage that a small selection of raw food is sufficient to create a large variety of substantial dishes.

For example, five substantial meals for four people or an impressive spread for about ten people can be made with a large leg of mutton, ten tomatoes, ten zucchini, crushed wheat, rice, a few eggs, nuts, spices and herbs. To do this, the leg of mutton is boned and a broth made with the bones. The lean part of the meat is then minced and mixed with crushed wheat to make two varieties of kibbi, the national dish. The remainder of the meat is chopped and ground. Half of it is mixed with nuts and used as a filling for the tomatoes. The remaining meat, mixed with rice, is used to stuff scooped-out zucchini. And the scooped out pulp of the zucchini, combined with eggs, makes tasty fritters. These dishes are then served as required, with rice or Bur'ghul Pilaf and the usual accompaniments of yoghurt, salad vegetables, bread and olives.

The cook always endeavours to present food with a flavour that appeals to most palates and does not require additional seasoning at the table. Spices, herbs and natural flavourings are an integral part of most recipes, but as a rule they are not used overpoweringly.

The most widely used spices are nutmeg, cinnamon, cloves, various peppers, coriander, cumin, aniseed and gum arabic. Popular herbs are mint, parsley, sesame seeds, thyme, marjoram and sim'meh. Flavourings include garlic, onions, lemons, olive oil, ghee, tomatoes, pine nuts, almonds, rosewater and orange blossom water.

The main meal in Lebanon is usually served in the evening, but on weekends and public holidays it may be eaten at midday. A main meal is always served when guests come to the house, whatever the time of day.

At the beginning of the main meal, mezza (hors d'oeuvres) are served with drinks. Mezza consists of a large variety of nuts, pickles, cheese and other foods, displayed in small dishes from which it is picked up with the fingers.

Mezza is an important part of Lebanese social life. It is a leisurely, relaxing period in which eating and drinking is accompanied by congenial conversation or a game of torlie (backgammon). As the time taken up for mezza can extend to three hours or more, the main course will often be served at a very late hour. Sometimes, particularly during holidays or in restaurants, an elaborate mezza will take the place of a full meal.

Alcoholic beverages are never served without the accompaniment of at least a few mezza dishes. The main alcoholic beverage is arack, a grape extract flavoured with aniseed. Various wines, spirits and beers are also popular.

Traditionally only water is served with the main course, confining alcoholic drinks to the predinner mezza period. However, today arack, wine or beer is often poured at the table or after a meal.

At least three dishes are served for the main course of the main meal. On important occasions, such as when guests are present or during a celebration, many more dishes are presented.

The main course usually consists of a meat, a cooked vegetable, and a grain dish, together with the usual accompaniment of yoghurt, salad, bread and olives. The food is placed on serving platters or in bowls on the centre of the table, and those at the table serve themselves, taking small portions of each variety of food or choosing larger portions of one or two dishes only.

At the completion of the main course, fresh or dried fruits are placed in the centre of the table and coffee is

served, sometimes accompanied with sweet pastries or puddings.

Lebanese coffee is the strong Turkish variety with a thick sediment. It is served often and, like mezza, is an important part of the Lebanese way of life. Visitors are always offered a cup of coffee, no matter what time of day or night, but a second cup is not offered at the same serving.

The average person probably drinks 6–10 cups of coffee each day. These cups are tiny (smaller than demitasse) and the sediment is left in the bottom, so the daily coffee consumption does not amount to more than that in Western countries.

Traditionally, sweet coffee is served during festive times and bitter coffee is made for sad occasions.

Breakfast always includes coffee, bread and some of the following foods: black olives, cheese, zaatar (a herb mixture), eggs, fresh or dried fruit and jam.

A light meal is generally a bowl of soup or a cooked vegetable or grain dish, with accompaniments such as cheese, olives, salad vegetables and yoghurt. Sandwiches made from Lebanese bread are also very popular.

The following menus are examples of a typical Lebanese diet.

Breakfast

1. Cream Cheese
Zaatar Mixture
Black Olives—Bread
Coffee
Fresh Fruit

2. Eggs Fried in Olive Oil
Zaatar Mixture
Black Olives—Bread
Coffee
Jams

3. White Cheese
Black Olives—Bread
Coffee
Dried Fruits

Lunch

1. Kibbi Balls in Yoghurt
Bread—Olives—Cheese
Jams

2. Dried Beans with Onions
or Green Beans in Oil
Spring Onions—Radish—Bread
Fresh Fruit

3. Cold Baked Kibbi in Oil
Salad—Yoghurt—Olives—Pickles—Bread
Rice Pudding

4. Bean and Grain Soup
or Bur'ghul and Lentil Soup
Raw Onions—Radish—Olives
Dried Fruit

5. Lentil and Rice Pilaf
Fattoush
Radish—Olives—Spring Onions
Fresh Fruit

Dinner

1. Mezza
A selection of hors d'oeuvres and drinks

Main Course:
Baked Stuffed Kibbi Loaf
Stuffed Eggplants
Green Bean Stew
Rice Pilaf
Salad—Olives—Bread

Coffee
Dried Fruits and Jams

2. Mezza
A selection of hors d'oeuvres and drinks

Main Course:
Chicken and Rice Soup
Baked Kibbi Shells
Okra Stew
Bur'ghul Pilaf
Yoghurt—Olives—Salad—Bread

Coffee
Fresh Fruit
Sweet Pastries

3. Mezza
A selection of hors d'oeuvres and drinks

Main Course:
Kafta on Skewers
Lahem Mishwi
Kibbi Nayye
Grape Vine Leaf Rolls
Hoummus b'Tahini
Tabbouleh
Olives—Bread

Coffee
Dried Fruits—Rice Pudding

4. Mezza
A selection of hors d'oeuvres and drinks

Main Course:
Baked Peppered Fish
Small Fried Fish
Spicy Rice for Fish
Tahini Sauce
Fried Bread Pieces
Fried cauliflower
Eggplant and Potatoes
Salad—Olives

Coffee
Fresh Fruit

ingredients

Bur'ghul

Bur'ghul is a crushed wheat which has been boiled, dried in the sun and then ground. It can be obtained from health food stores and delicatessens under the names of "bur'ghul" or "Lebanese crushed wheat"—do not use ordinary cracked wheat. The quantities given in the recipes refer to the dried grain, however it will swell up when you wash and drain it.

Dried beans (and dried peas)

Dried beans should always be soaked before cooking. The best way to do this is to soak them overnight in a large bowl with three times their amount of cold water and a pinch of bicarbonate of soda. However, if you are in a hurry you can reduce the time by omitting the bicarbonate of soda and bringing the beans and water to a boil, boiling for 2 minutes, then turning off the heat and allowing to stand for 1 hour.

When you are ready to cook the beans, drain off the water in which they were soaked, replace it with three times their amount of fresh water and bring to a boil. Cover and simmer strongly, stirring occasionally, until the water is well reduced, about 20–30 minutes. Turn down the heat and simmer slowly, adding more water if necessary, until tender (test by pressing a bean between the fingers). Be careful not to overcook the beans.

Eggplants

Prepare all varieties of eggplants for cooking by peeling, scooping, chopping or slicing as directed in the recipe. Then sprinkle with salt and allow to drain in a colander for at least 30 minutes or, alternatively, soak in salted water for 1 hour. Drain and dry with a towel or paper towels. These procedures eliminate the eggplants' bitter characteristic and tendency to absorb a great deal of oil during cooking.

Herbs

Fresh, dried and powdered herbs are used in Lebanese cooking. If you run out of one type it can be substituted by another in the following proportions: 1 tablespoon fresh chopped herbs = 1 teaspoon dried = $1/2$ teaspoon powdered.

Many Lebanese cooks prefer to dry their own herbs, particularly parsley and mint. The method for drying is: Wash and dry the fresh herb. Tie it in a bunch, then hang it upside-down in a draughty place for several weeks until the leaves crumble easily in the hand. Remove the leaves from the stem and crush

Most of the ingredients and equipment used in the Lebanese kitchen will be familiar to the Western cook, however in some instances the food is prepared differently. The following list contains all you need to know about the basic ingredients and equipment used throughout this book. Directions for specific areas are contained in the relevant chapters.

Bur'ghul

Dried chick peas

Eggplants (Lebanese variety pictured)

Herbs

Hot peppers

Hoummus

Lentils

Mixed spices

Peppers

Pine nuts

the leaves to a powder by rubbing them in the palms of the hands. Store in an airtight jar.

Hot peppers
"Necklaces" of dried red and green hot peppers (chillies) decorate most Lebanese kitchens. They can be used instead of fresh ones in all recipes, provided they are soaked first in hot water until they become soft. The method for drying is: Wash and dry the hot peppers. Using a large needle and strong thread, sew through the stems to make a "necklace". Hang the necklace in a draughty place until the peppers are completely dried.

Hoummus
Hoummus means chick peas. The dip popularly known as "hoummus" is correctly Hoummus b'Tahini.

Lentils
Before cooking lentils it is advisable to spread them out on a tray and inspect them for pieces of grit, then wash well and drain. They do not need soaking.

Mixed spices
Spices are generally mixed for use in Lebanese cooking. Where a recipe states mixed spices, you can use the commercial "mixed spice" (which combines allspice, cinnamon, nutmeg and cinnamon oil) or blend your own mixture. Note that "allspice" (pimento) is a reddish brown berry which tastes like a mixture of cinnamon, cloves, nutmeg and juniper and should not be mistaken for mixed spice.

Another popular spice mixture in Lebanon is "four spice", a combination of cinnamon nutmeg, cloves and ginger. A favourite pepper mixture is made up of 2 parts allspice, 2 parts black pepper and 1 part white pepper.

Peppers
The red and green peppers (capsicum) used in all recipes must be fresh.

Pine nuts
These are the kernels from the cones of the stone or umbrella pine (Pinus pinea), a native of the Mediterranean region. They have a distinctive flavour and can be purchased from supermarkets, health food shops and delicatessens. Blanched slivered almonds are a suitable substitute in most recipes.

Pomegranates

Pomegranates are a popular and plentiful fruit in the Middle East. The fresh fruit is used for decorating food and a special pomegranate sauce called Dibbis Rhuman is often used for flavouring savoury dishes. This sauce is available at some Lebanese food shops, but as it is not readily procurable elsewhere we have used lemon juice in this book.

Rosewater and orange blossom water

The rosewater and orange blossom water used in this book are the diluted essences available from chemists, drug stores, health food shops and some continental delicatessens. Pure essence, which is much more expensive, may be substituted but the quantities should be reduced to a few drops.

Tahini

Tahini is a white, slightly bitter sesame paste made from raw sesame seeds. It can be obtained from delicatessens and health food stores and will keep indefinitely. Do not confuse it with the brown, nutty sesame paste made from roasted sesame seeds, which is sold at Asian stores.

Tomato paste

Commercial tomato paste can be used for the recipes in this book, however most Lebanese prefer to use this homemade paste. For a yield of about 1 lb (500 g): Wash 5 lb (2.5 kg) ripe tomatoes, core out the stem ends and slice into a large pot. Cover and heat gently until soft, then rub through a sieve. Return the juice to the pot and simmer slowly, uncovered, until reduced by half to a tomato purée. Pour into a baking dish, cover with gauze and dry in the sun for 2–4 days, stirring occasionally. (Alternatively, cook in a cool oven for 4–6 hours.) When the tomatoes are the consistency of a soft paste, stir in 1 tablespoon of salt and spoon into sterilised jars. Pour a layer of oil on top, seal and store in a cool place. When opened, store in the refrigerator.

Zaatar mixture

This is a popular herbal blend consisting of 1 part thyme (zaatar), 1 part roasted sesame seeds, 1/2 part sim'meh and salt to taste. It can be bought from most Lebanese delicatessens. Thyme is a suitable substitute.

Pomegranates

Rosewater and orange blossom water

Tahini

Tomato paste

Zaatar mixture

Mincer

Mortar and pestle

Rakweh

Sorj

Zucchini scoop

Mincer

A simple mincer (grinder) will be very helpful for preparing many ingredients.

Mortar and pestle

A mortar is a vessel in which food is pounded with a pestle. A milk bottle and bread board or rolling pin and bread board are suitable substitutes. Unless otherwise stated, you can use a blender if you prefer.

Rakweh

A traditional Lebanese coffee pot, made from copper or aluminium, which features a long handle. A small saucepan with a pouring lip is a suitable substitute.

Sorj

A sorj is a simple convex metal plate measuring between 12 in (30 cm) and 36 in (90 cm), used when making Bread Cloth. It can be purchased at Lebanese or Indian stores.

Zucchini scoop

To scoop out zucchini and eggplant for stuffing, a special utensil called ma'warra is used. This scoop can be purchased from Lebanese importers, or you can make your own using the following method: Cut a 12-in (30-cm) piece of 1/2-in (12-mm) copper pipe in a lengthwise slope down the middle, so that you have a cut section of 7 in (18 cm) with an uncut section of 5 in (12 cm) which can be used as a handle. Sharpen all the cut edges. An apple corer may be used as a substitute.

basic mixtures

Basic mixtures of rice, stuffings, yoghurts, cheese, sauces, pastries and bread form the foundation of all Lebanese cooking. At least one is included in every meal, often as part of another recipe.

The beauty of this style of cooking is that a large amount of food can be made and then stored ready for future meals. This is extremely useful if you intend to eat Lebanese food for a few days or if you are planning a large dinner party and want to get as much work as possible done ahead of time.

Study these recipes well and practise making them, for once they are familiar you will find Lebanese cooking very simple.

Tahini sauce Taratoor b'tahini

Makes 2¼ cups   **V**   **L**

1 clove garlic
½ teaspoon salt
1 cup tahini (see page 16)
about ½ cup lemon juice
water
½ cup finely chopped parsley (optional)

Crush the garlic and salt together to a paste. Mix in the tahini and beat in the lemon juice. Gradually mix in enough water to make the mixture the consistency of very thick cream or mayonnaise. Add parsley if using, and adjust salt and lemon to taste.

Pine nut sauce Taratoor b'snoobar

This sauce is traditionally served with fish.

Makes approx ¾ cup   **V**

1 slice of soft ordinary bread (not the Lebanese variety) without crust, ½ in (1.25 cm) thick and soaked in 1 cup water
1 clove garlic
½ tablespoon salt
¾ cup pine nuts
about ½ cup lemon juice
2 tablespoons water

Squeeze the soaked bread to remove water. Crush the garlic and salt together. Pound in the pine nuts to a paste. Pound in the bread, add the lemon juice and water. Sieve the mixture through a fine strainer. Adjust salt and lemon to taste.

Alternative method Place all the ingredients into a blender and blend into a smooth sauce, adding more water if necessary.

Avocado with tahini sauce
Taratoor b'abocarto

Makes about 2 cups   **V**   **L**

1 large avocado
³/₄ cup Tahini Sauce (see page 18)

Peel and mash the avocado and blend in the Tahini Sauce until smooth. Adjust lemon and salt to taste, if necessary.

Serve with salad vegetables or as a dip for mezza.

Garlic sauce Zait b'toom

Garlic sauce is a delicious accompaniment for grilled chicken or shellfish. It is extremely important that you start crushing the garlic with a mortar and pestle to ensure that the oil will be thoroughly absorbed. Do not add the oil or lemon juice too quickly and always stir in one direction only or the mixture will fall flat.

Makes about 2¹/₂ cups   **V**   **L**

all cloves of 1 knob of garlic
1 teaspoon salt
about 2 cups olive oil
about ¹/₄ cup lemon juice

Crush garlic in the salt with a mortar and pestle until the salt is dissolved. Very gradually add 1 tablespoon of oil (a few drops at a time) and then a few drops of lemon juice and, stirring in one direction with the pestle, blend into the garlic. When the oil has been completely absorbed into the garlic, very gradually add another tablespoon of oil alternately with a few more drops of lemon juice, continuing until the oil is no longer being absorbed into the garlic (after gradually adding four tablespoons you may use an electric blender). The mixture should be light and fluffy like whipped cream. If it is not, you can save the day by mixing in a well-mashed potato.

Ghee Sumneh

Ghee is clarified butter. It can be purchased commercially or made at home. Ordinary butter, margarine or nut or vegetable oil may be substituted, but ghee has a distinctive flavour and does not burn easily. Unlike butter or margarine, it keeps indefinitely unrefrigerated.

Makes 2 lb (1 kg)   **V**
Cooking time about 20 minutes

2 lb (1 kg) butter

Place butter in a large saucepan, melt and bring to a boil. Allow to boil for a few minutes, watching very carefully. As soon as the froth on the surface starts to disperse, remove immediately from heat and allow to cool. Skim off the remainder of froth.

Pour into a glass or earthenware jar, being careful not to pour in the sediment on the bottom of the pan.

Thick clotted cream Ushta

Ushta is the thick layer of clotted cream from the top of rich, boiled goats milk. Unlike whipped cream it does not melt when cooked or served with hot sweets. A substitute can be made with cows milk and cream using this recipe.

Makes 2½ pints (1.25 L)   **V**
Cooking time about 1½ hours

2 pints (1 L) milk
½ pint (250 ml) cream

Mix the milk and cream together and place in a wide shallow tray on top of the stove. Bring slowly to a boil, then turn down the heat as low as possible and allow the mixture to stand over it for 30 minutes.

Turn off the heat, cover and leave the mixture to stand for 8 hours before refrigerating. Place in the refrigerator for a further 7 hours. With a sharp knife, detach the thick layer of cream from around the edges of the pan and lift it off the top of the milk. Place the cream on a platter and slice it into pieces.

Yoghurt Lubban

In Lebanese cuisine yoghurt is served in a variety of ways, but never with fish or tahini. When preparing yoghurt, temperature conditions must be exactly right and the culture must not be disturbed while it is working.

Makes 5 cups   **V**
Cooking time about 20 minutes

1 cup full-cream powdered milk
5 cups whole milk (not homogenised)
1 tablespoon plain yoghurt (for starter)

Mix the powdered milk into the fresh milk in a saucepan and heat until it comes to a boil. When boiled immediately remove from the heat and leave to cool until lukewarm. The mixture should be just warm enough for the yoghurt germ to spread (97°F/36°C). (The traditional way to test this temperature is to immerse the little finger in the milk. You should be able to hold it there for the count of ten, but no longer.)

In a large cup, mix several tablespoons of the warm milk with the starter yoghurt and stir to a smooth paste. Add the paste to the remainder of the warm milk, and stir in gently. Pour the mixture into an enamel or porcelain bowl, cover with a lid or plate, wrap a towel (in summer) or blanket (in winter) around it and allow to stand in a warm place for 6 hours or until set. Remove towel or blanket and refrigerate.

The yoghurt will set like a junket. The taste will vary according to the age of the starter: if the starter is refrigerated for a week or more the yoghurt will be very tart; if the starter is fresh it will be sweeter.

Variation Yoghurt can also be made using instant powdered milk instead of full-cream milk and whole milk. Use 2½ cups of very hot water (not boiling) for every 1½ cups of instant powdered milk. Place them in a bowl and mix well. Test temperature, mix in starter, cover and set aside as above.

Cooked yoghurt Luggan mutboukh

Makes 2½ pints (1.25 L)   **V**
Cooking time 20 minutes

2 pints (1.25 L) yoghurt
1 egg white, beaten
2 cloves garlic, crushed
1 teaspoon salt
1 tablespoon dried mint or coriander
2 heaped teaspoons cornflour/cornstarch (optional)

In a saucepan beat together yoghurt and beaten egg white. Bring to a boil slowly, stirring constantly in the same direction (this avoids burning or curdling).

When the yoghurt comes to a boil add the crushed garlic cloves, salt and dried mint or coriander. If a thicker consistency is required, mix 2 heaped teaspoons of cornflour/cornstarch to a paste with water and blend into the mixture just before it comes to the boil.

White cheese Jibni byda

Makes ½ lb (250 g)   **V**
Cooking time 5 minutes

5 pints (2.5 L) milk (not homogenised)
1 plain junket tablet, dissolved in 1 tablespoon cold water
1 tablespoon salt

Heat milk until it is just slightly warm. Stir in the dissolved junket tablet and the salt. Leave it to stand uncovered in a warm place until set, about 20 minutes.

Break up curds with a large spoon, pour into a colander lined with cheesecloth and place in the sink. Stir mixture for a few minutes so that the curds separate and the whey drains through the cloth.

When most of the whey has drained off, tie the corners of the cloth into a sack. Return the sack to the colander and set it over a bowl or hang it from a tap over the kitchen sink.

When the whey has completely drained away and the curds become a solid mass (about 1–2 hours), turn out into a shallow bowl. Sprinkle with more salt if necessary. Cover and store in refrigerator.

Cream cheese Lubbneh

Lubbneh is a favourite Lebanese breakfast when served with olive oil, zaatar mixture (see page 16), olives and bread.

Makes about ¼ of original quantity of yoghurt   **V**

Place a quantity of cold yoghurt in cheesecloth or similar material, tie the corners of the cloth into a sack and hang it on the kitchen tap to allow liquid to drain into the sink. Alternatively hang over a bowl.

Remove the cheese from cloth after 8 hours. Sprinkle with salt and store in a covered container in refrigerator.

Use as a spread or mould into little balls.

Meat and nut filling Hashweh

Makes 2 cups
Cooking time 35 minutes

3 tablespoons ghee or substitute (see page 19)
$1/2$ cup pine nuts
1 lb (500 g) meat, coarsely ground or finely chopped
2 medium onions, finely chopped
2 teaspoons salt
$1/4$ teaspoon pepper
$1/4$ teaspoon mixed spices (see page 15)
$1/4$ teaspoon ground cinnamon

Heat the ghee in a pan and lightly brown the pine nuts. Remove and set aside.

Add the meat to the ghee and fry for a few minutes until the raw look disappears. Before the meat browns, mix in the chopped onions, salt, pepper, mixed spices and cinnamon. Cover, turn down to medium heat and continue to cook until meat is very tender and the juices are absorbed, about 20–25 minutes.

Remove from heat and mix in the pine nuts.

Meat and rice stuffing Hashwit mihshi

Makes 4 cups
Cooking time 10 minutes

1 medium onion, finely chopped
1 tablespoon ghee or substitute (see page 19)
2 teaspoons salt
1 teaspoon black pepper
1 teaspoon ground cinnamon or mixed spices (see page 15)
$1^{1}/4$ cups rice, washed and drained
1 lb (500 g) coarsely ground or finely chopped meat
  (preferably lamb shoulder)
$1/2$ cup water

Sauté onion in the ghee until soft. Mix onion and ghee, salt, pepper and cinnamon into rice. Add the meat and water. Mix well. This stuffing is used for vegetables.

Lenten stuffing Hashwi orteh

This stuffing contains no meat or dairy products and is ideal for vegetarian dishes. It can supplement the filling in all stuffed vegetables, however when used for stuffed tomatoes, omit the chick peas.

Makes 4 cups   **V**   **L**

$1/2$ cup chick peas, soaked overnight (see page 14)
$1/2$ cup chopped mint or 2 teaspoons dried mint
$1/2$ cup finely chopped parsley
2 medium tomatoes, chopped
$1/2$ cup chopped spring onions
$1^{1}/4$ cups rice, washed and drained
1 teaspoon salt
$1/4$ teaspoon ground cinnamon
$1/4$ teaspoon pepper
$1/4$ teaspoon zaatar mixture (see page 16) or thyme (optional)
1 cup olive or nut oil
3 tablespoons lemon juice

Drain the soaked chick peas and crack them by placing in a clean cloth and rolling with a rolling pin.

Wash and drain the cracked chick peas, place in a bowl and mix in all the remaining ingredients.

Bur'ghul pilaf Bur'ghul b'dfeen

Serves 6–8   **V**
Cooking time 50 minutes

2 cups bur'ghul, washed and drained (see page 14)
1^1/$_4$ cups pine nuts to garnish (optional)
^{1}/$_2$ cup ghee or substitute (see page 19)
1 medium onion, chopped
2 teaspoons salt
^{1}/$_4$ teaspoon black pepper
3^1/$_2$ cups meat or chicken broth

Wash the bur'ghul and drain well by squeezing out excess water between cupped hands. Place in a bowl and set aside for 30 minutes or more.

In a large saucepan, lightly fry pine nuts, if using, in half the ghee, drain and set aside. Fry onion in the same ghee until golden brown. Add the remainder of the ghee, heat and stir in bur'ghul, salt and pepper. Sauté for a few minutes.

In another saucepan, bring the broth to a boil and mix it into the bur'ghul mixture. Allow to bubble for a few seconds. Cover tightly, turn down the heat and simmer very slowly—or place in the oven as a casserole at 350°F (180°C/Gas 4).

The pilaf is cooked when all the stock has been absorbed and the bur'ghul is soft and fluffy, about 40–50 minutes. (If the stock is absorbed before the bur'ghul is cooked, add a little more boiling stock or water and continue cooking.) Allow to stand for at least 15 minutes. Serve in place of rice and garnish with pine nuts.

Variations Three peeled and chopped tomatoes may be added with the broth but reduce the broth by ^{1}/$_2$ cup. Chopped spring onions may be added with the broth.

Rice pilaf Ruz bi-shaireeyeh

Serves 6–8   **V**
Cooking time 30 minutes

1 cup broken-up vermicelli or fine egg noodles
2^1/$_2$ tablespoons ghee or substitute (see page 19)
2 cups rice (preferably long grain), washed and drained
1^1/$_2$ teaspoons salt
4 cups boiling water
ground cinnamon

Sauté the vermicelli or noodles in the ghee until a light brown colour, stirring constantly to avoid burning. Mix the rice and salt well into the vermicelli then add the boiling water. Give one final stir, allow a few seconds to bubble, then cover the rice tightly. Turn down heat to very low and simmer until cooked, about 20 minutes.

When ready to serve, stir the rice gently with a fork, turn onto serving dish and sprinkle ground cinnamon lightly over the top.

Variations Lightly fried pine nuts may also be sprinkled over the rice. When served with chicken, half chicken broth may be substituted for half the amount of water. Alternatively add 2 chicken stock cubes to the water.

Lebanese bread Khoubiz

Makes 8 rounds   **V**   **L**
Cooking time 4–8 minutes per round

¹/₂ oz (15 g) dried yeast or 1 oz (30 g) fresh yeast
2¹/₂ cups lukewarm water
1 teaspoon sugar
8 cups plain flour
2 teaspoons salt
3 tablespoons oil

Dissolve the yeast in ¹/₄ cup of the lukewarm water, add sugar and set aside in a warm place until it rises and foams, about 10–15 minutes.

Sift the flour and salt into a large mixing bowl and place in a warm oven for a few minutes to warm slightly.

Pour the yeast into a well in the centre of the flour and mix it in by hand, adding the water gradually. Knead well to a soft dough. Turn the dough onto a lightly floured board or cloth and continue to knead until it is smooth and shiny, about 15–20 minutes.

Knead in 2 tablespoons of the oil, roll into a large ball and rub the remainder of the oil around the ball. Place in the bowl, cover with a damp cloth and set aside in a warm place to rise until nearly double size, about 1–2 hours. Turn the oven on to maximum heat at least 45 minutes before cooking the bread.

Punch down the dough in the centre and draw edges to the middle to re-form the ball. Turn onto a floured board or cloth and knead for about 2 minutes.

Divide the dough into 8 equal portions and roll each into a ball. Flatten each ball on a lightly floured cloth and roll with a rolling pin into flat round shapes, about the size of a dinner plate and about ¹/₄ in (6 mm) thick. Place rounds on a floured cloth, cover with another floured cloth and set aside again to rise to nearly double in size, about 20–30 minutes. Place a baking tray in oven for 5 minutes, remove and lightly rub with oil.

Place 1 round of bread on the baking tray and bake until it swells up in the centre and browns slightly, about 4–8 minutes. Remove from oven and wrap in a cloth. Continue until all the rounds are cooked.

The bread should be white, soft and chewy. When cut in half, it will form a pocket into which sandwich fillings of every description may be placed.

Bread cloth Khoubiz sorj

To make this recipe you will require a sorj. This is a simple convex metal plate measuring between 12 in (30 cm) and 36 in (90 cm), which can be purchased at Lebanese or Indian stores. An substitute is an old plough disc.

Makes 8–16 rounds, depending on sorj size   **V**   **L**
Cooking time 3–5 minutes per round

2 lb (1 kg) Lebanese Bread dough (see left)

Follow recipe as for Lebanese Bread. After the dough has risen, divide it into about 16 small balls, depending on the size of the sorj.

With a rolling pin, roll out each ball as thinly as possible on a floured cloth. It is not necessary to keep an absolutely round shape but it should be as thin as cloth and have no holes in it. Place the sorj convexly (domelike) over a hotplate. When very hot, carefully lift the cloth bread onto it. Leave until cooked through and forming bubbles, about 3–5 minutes. Peel the bread off the sorj and continue the process until all the bread is cooked.

This bread is used to roll up sandwich fillings of any description.

mezza

Mezza is a selection of hors d'oeuvres, often comprising thirty or more small dishes. It is traditionally served as an appetiser, but is sometimes eaten as a meal in itself. Arack, an anisated alcoholic drink, is always served with the mezza, along with Lebanese bread, which can be torn into small pieces for the dips.

The "home of mezza" is the town of Zahle, situated in the picturesque countryside at the foot of Mount Lebanon. Here the best quality arack is produced and an amazing number of restaurants specialise in mezza.

To make up a mezza you may choose a selection of kibbi, cheese, nuts, raisins, pickles, olives, dips, Tabbouleh (see page 96) and other salads, grape vine rolls, various savoury pastries and any of the following recipes.

Fried eggplant Batinjaan mi'li

Makes 1 mezza dish   **V**   **L**
Cooking time 10–15 minutes

1 medium eggplant
olive or nut oil, for frying
salt and pepper
juice of 1 lemon

Peel the eggplant, slice into ¼-in (5-mm) circles and prepare for cooking (see page 14).

Fry sliced eggplant in oil until browned on both sides and soft inside. Drain on paper towels.

Sprinkle with salt, pepper and lemon juice, and serve warm or cold with bread.

Eggplant and tahini dip Baba ghannouj

Makes 1 mezza dish   **V**   **L**
Cooking time 20 minutes

1 large eggplant
about ¼ cup lemon juice
4–5 tablespoons tahini (see page 16)
2 cloves garlic
1½ teaspoons salt
¼ cup finely chopped parsley for garnish

Remove the green from around the neck of the eggplant, but leave the stem. Place in a preheated hot oven until soft, about 15–20 minutes—or hold onto stem and place over open grill or hotplate, turning from time to time until eggplant has softened. Allow to cool.

Remove the skin carefully, while holding the stem. Mash pulp thoroughly with a fork or place in the blender then slowly beat in lemon juice alternately with tahini.

Crush garlic with salt and mix to a paste. Blend into the eggplant mixture. Adjust salt.

Pour into shallow serving dishes or platters and garnish with chopped parsley. Serve with Lebanese bread.

Chick pea dip Hoummus b'Tahini

Makes about cups   **V**   **L**
Cooking time about 1½ hours

1½ cups chick peas, soaked overnight (see page 14)
water
2 teaspoons salt
about 2 cloves garlic
¼ cup tahini (see page 16)
about ½ cup lemon juice
pinch cayenne pepper and 2 tablespoons chopped parsley for
  garnish

Drain the soaked chick peas, place in a pot and add three times their amount of water. Add 1 teaspoon salt and bring to a boil. Boil vigorously for about 10 minutes, turn down the heat, cover the saucepan and simmer until the chick peas are very soft, about 1 hour. Drain liquid and reserve. Reserve ½ cup of the whole, cooked chick peas for garnish. Purée the remainder of the chick peas by pressing through a sieve or placing in blender.

Crush the garlic with the remaining teaspoon of salt. Beat or blend it into the purée.

Slowly beat in the tahini and lemon juice alternately. Blend in a little of the reserved liquid to make the mixture a thick creamy consistency. Adjust salt and lemon to taste.

Serve on a platter garnished with a pinch of cayenne pepper, parsley and the reserved chick peas.

Fried cauliflower Ar'nabit mi'li

Makes 1 mezza dish   **V**   **L**
Cooking time about 20 minutes

1 small cauliflower
olive or nut oil, for frying
salt and pepper
juice of 1 lemon

Separate the cauliflower in flowerettes and deep-fry in oil until golden brown and tender. Drain on paper towels.

Sprinkle with salt, pepper and lemon juice. Serve warm or cold.

Fried chicken giblets in lemon juice
Bearsheart mi'leeyeh

Makes 1 mezza dish
Cooking time 25 minutes

2 cups chicken giblets
2 tablespoons ghee or substitute (see page 19)
2 medium onions, finely chopped
2 cloves garlic, crushed
salt
pepper
½ teaspoon mixed spices (see page 15)
juice of 1 lemon
¼ cup finely chopped parsley for garnish

Wash the giblets, then sauté in hot ghee until brown and nearly cooked through, about 15 minutes. Add the chopped onions and garlic and continue to sauté until the onions are soft. Mix in the salt, pepper and mixed spices, then the lemon juice and sauté for a few more minutes.

Serve warm or cold, garnished with parsley.

Fried kidneys in lemon juice
Kar'laerwe mi'leeyeh

Makes 1 mezza dish
Cooking time ½ hour

12 lamb kidneys or 5 beef kidneys
salt and pepper
½ cup ghee or substitute (see page 19)
2 tablespoons plain flour
½ cup lemon juice
1 teaspoon dried mint

Wash and dry kidneys. Split lengthwise and remove skin. Flatten with a pestle or rolling pin and sprinkle with salt and pepper. Melt ghee in a pan and fry kidneys until brown on both sides. Remove kidneys from the pan and set aside.

Add flour to pan, lower heat and stir until it begins to turn brown. Add lemon juice and bring to a boil. Return kidneys to pan, add dried mint and allow to simmer in the sauce for a few minutes.

Marinated lambs' brains N'kha m'tabbal

Makes 1 mezza dish
Cooking time 10–15 minutes

6 sets lambs' brains
salt
water
1 teaspoon vinegar
lemon wedge
¼ cup olive oil
½ cup lemon juice
½ cup chopped spring onions
pepper
¼ cup finely chopped parsley for garnish

If brains are fresh, remove skin (this is easier if soaked for 30 minutes in cold water, a little salt and 1 tablespoon of vinegar). If brains are frozen, leave unskinned as the skin will be too difficult to remove.

Simmer brains gently in salted water with 1 teaspoon of vinegar and 1 lemon wedge until tender, about 10–15 minutes. Drain well and let cool.

Cut brains into narrow strips and place in a small serving dish. Make a mixture with the olive oil, lemon juice, spring onions and pepper. Adjust salt. Pour over the brains, garnish with chopped parsley and refrigerate.

Serve chilled.

Marinated tongue salad L'sanaat m'tabli

Makes 1 mezza dish
Cooking time 2½ hours

4 sheeps' tongues or 1 small beef tongue
1 large carrot, finely chopped
1 large onion, finely chopped
2 spring onions, finely chopped
1 teaspoon salt
1 cup water
½ cup lemon juice
¼ cup olive oil
1 clove garlic crushed in ½ teaspoon salt
½ cup finely chopped parsley for garnish

Place the tongues in a saucepan, cover with cold water and bring to a boil. Turn down the heat and simmer for 1½ hours.

Drain off water, remove skin from tongues and chop into pieces. Place in saucepan with carrot, onion, spring onions, salt and water. Bring to a boil, turn down the heat and simmer until tender.

Drain liuid from saucepan and place tongues and vegetables into a serving bowl.

Make a dressing with the lemon juice, oil and garlic crushed in salt. Pour over the tongues and vegetables, garnish with parsley and refrigerate.

Serve chilled.

Fried lamb's liver Kibid mi'li

Makes 1 mezza dish
Cooking time 15–20 minutes

1 lamb's fry/liver
½ cup olive or nut oil
salt and pepper
juice of 1 lemon
1 tablespoon chopped parsley for garnish

Cut the lamb's fry into 1-in (2.5-cm) strips, discarding the gristle. Fry in hot oil to brown the outside and lightly cook inside. Chop into cubes and serve warm or cold sprinkled with lemon juice and garnished with parsley.

savoury pastries

Savoury pastries are a popular feature of Lebanese cuisine. They come in a variety of shapes and sizes, and the fillings are almost limitless.

We have selected the traditional pastry recipes. They are surprisingly easy to make and can be varied in size, shape and filling as desired.

Savoury pastries are excellent for mezza or light snacks, but may also be served as part of the main course. They are best when piping hot, but are still delicious warm. Whichever way you serve them, make sure they are plentiful because they always disappear quickly!

Simple pastry

This is the traditional Lebanese savoury pastry. However, any commercial or homemade bread dough or filo pastry may be substituted.

Makes 1 lb (500 g)   **V**

2¹/₂ cups self-raising flour
¹/₂ teaspoon salt
2 tablespoons ghee or substitute (see page 19)
about ³/₄ cup water

Sift the flour and salt together and rub in the ghee. Add the water gradually to make a soft dough. Knead until smooth, adding more water if necessary.

Cover with a damp cloth and place in refrigerator for 30 minutes before rolling out.

Fried meat and pine nut pies Sambousik

Makes 30 small pies
Cooking time 3–4 minutes each

2 cups Meat and Nut Filling (see page 22)
about 2 tablespoons lemon juice
about 2 tablespoons vinegar
1 lb (500 g) Simple Pastry (see above)
olive oil or substitute

Place the Meat and Nut Filling in a bowl and mix in the lemon juice and vinegar. Roll out the pastry to about ¹/₈ in (3 mm) thick. Cut into small rounds about 3 in (7.5 cm) in diameter.

Place 1¹/₂ teaspoons of filling on each pastry round and fold over the pastry to form a semicircle shape. Pinch the edges firmly together.

Deep-fry in oil until golden. Serve piping hot.

2

3

Meat pastry rolls Lahem b'ajeen

Makes 30
Cooking time 15 minutes

2 cups Meat and Nut Filling (see page 22)
about 2 tablespoons vinegar
about 2 tablespoons lemon juice
1 lb (500 g) Simple Pastry (see 32)
¼ cup ghee or substitute (see page 19)

1. Place the Meat and Nut Filling in a bowl and mix in the vinegar and lemon juice. Take one small ball of pastry at a time and roll into a thin sheet on a floured board. Cut into strips about 3 in x 4 in (7.5 cm x 10 cm).

2. Place 2 teaspoons of filling along the centre of each pastry strip. Roll up firmly and place on a well-greased baking tray.

3. Brush the top of each roll with melted ghee and bake in a pre-heatedmoderately hot oven until golden.

Variations Instead of rolls, make tart shapes by cutting out small thin rounds of pastry with a biscuit cutter and pulling up and pinching the edges all around to form round shells.

• Add 2 tablespoons of tomato paste, ½ cup of well-strained, peeled, chopped tomatoes and 2 tablespoons of parsley to the Meat and Nut Filling (extra salt may also be necessary).

• Substitute a mixture of 1¼ cups minced, steamed brains or cooked chicken, 1 tablespoon finely chopped parsley or spring onions, 1 unbeaten egg, salt and pepper for the Meat and Nut Filling.

• Substitute a mixture of 1¼ cups grated cheese, 1 tablespoon parsley and a pinch of cayenne pepper for the Meat and Nut Filling.

Spinach turnovers Fatayah b'sbaanegh

This recipe requires only the leaves of the spinach. Use the stalks for the salad recipe on page 99.

Makes 24 turnovers   **V**   **L**
Cooking time 20 minutes

2 lb (1 kg) Lebanese Bread dough (see page 25)
  or any commercial bread dough
olive or nut oi, for baking

FILLING
2 cups finely chopped spinach leaves
$^1/_2$ cup finely chopped parsley
$^1/_4$ cup finely chopped fresh mint or 1 teaspoon dried mint
$^1/_2$ cup finely chopped spring onions
$^1/_4$ cup pine nuts, lightly fried in olive oil (optional)
$1^1/_2$ teaspoons salt
$^1/_4$ teaspoon pepper
$^1/_4$ teaspoon mixed spices (see page 15)
$^1/_2$ teaspoon zaatar mixture (see page 16) or thyme
$^1/_4$ cup olive oil
about $^1/_4$ cup lemon juice

Place the bread dough in a warm place and allow to rise.

Mix all the filling ingredients together.

When the bread dough has risen, roll out on a floured board to $^1/_4$ in (6 mm) thick and cut into 4-in (10-cm) squares.

Place 1 tablespoon of filling on each square of dough and fold over to form a triangle-shape. Secure edges together by folding them over and pressing down firmly with fork prongs.

Place the pastries on a well-oiled baking tray and brush each one with oil. Bake in a preheated hot oven at 425°F (220°C/Gas 7) until lightly golden.

Serve hot or cold.

Herb rounds Mun'oosh b'zaatar

Makes 8 rounds   **V**   **L**
Cooking time 10–15 minutes per batch

2 lb (1 kg) Lebanese Bread dough (see page 25)
$^3/_4$ cup olive or nut oil
$^3/_4$ cup zaatar mixture (see page 16)

When the bread dough has risen, punch it down and knead again for 2 minutes. Divide it into 8 equal portions and roll each portion into a ball.

Flatten the dough balls on a floured cloth and using a rolling pin, roll into little rounds about the size of a small bread-and-butter plate and $^1/_2$-in (1.25-cm) thick. Place bread rounds on a lightly floured cloth, cover with another floured cloth and set aside to rise to nearly double their size—20–30 minutes. Make indents in the rounds by prodding with the finger. Pour oil over the surface and sprinkle liberally with zaatar mixture.

Bake in a preheated very hot oven at 500°F (250°C/Gas 10) until cooked, about 10–15 minutes.

These rounds should be very soft in texture so they can be eaten either rolled up or torn into pieces.

soups

Lebanese soups are very substantial. Rich with meat, grain, legumes and other vegetables, they are considered a meal in themselves but are sometimes served with a variety of dishes as part of the main course.

Like most parts of this cuisine, Lebanese soups keep well and the flavour is not spoiled by reheating. This is particularly useful in the cold winter months because a big cauldron of nourishing soup can always be on hand. The following soups are the most popular in Lebanon and include several Lenten recipes which use neither meat nor dairy products. Bread is always served with them.

Spinach soup Shourbet sbaanegh

Serves 4–6
Cooking time 1 hour plus 1½ hours for Basic Meat Broth

2½ pints (1.25 L) Basic Meat Broth plus meat (see page 43)
12 oz (360 g) Basic Kibbi Mixture (see page 56)
¼ cup ghee or substitute (see page 19)
1 medium onion, finely chopped
1 celery stalk, finely chopped
3 cloves garlic, crushed with salt
¼ cup rice, washed and drained
1 lb (500 g) spinach, finely chopped
salt

Remove meat from broth and set aside. Mould the kibbi into small balls and flatten into patties 1 in (2.5 cm) in diameter. Fry them in half the ghee, drain and set aside.

Brown the chopped onion in the remainder of the ghee, add the celery and garlic. Simmer this mixture for 2 minutes and stir it into the broth.

Bring broth to a boil, add the rice, and continue to simmer for 10 minutes. Bring back to a boil, add the kibbi patties, spinach and meat, and simmer for a further 10 minutes or until rice is cooked. Add salt to taste.

White bean soup Shourbet fassoolia byda

Serves 4–6
Cooking time 1 hour plus 1½ hours for Basic Meat
   Broth

1 lb (500 g) white beans, soaked overnight (see page 14)
2 spring onions
3 tablespoons ghee or substitute (see page 19)
2½ pints (1.25 L) Basic Meat Broth plus meat (see page
   43)
½ teaspoon salt

Boil the soaked beans for 30 minutes and drain.

Fry the spring onions in the ghee and add to the
broth along with the cooked, drained beans and salt.

Bring soup to a boil, cover and simmer until all the
ingredients are soft, about 30 minutes. Sieve or blend
into a purée. Adjust salt to taste. Reheat before serving.

Chicken and rice soup Shourbet djaaj b'ruz

**This is one of the lighter Lebanese soups and has a distinctly
lemony-garlic flavour.**

Serves 6–8
Cooking time 1¾ hours

1 large chicken, including giblets
3–4 celery stalks, chopped
2 leeks, sliced (optional)
2–3 cloves garlic, slivered
9 cups water
salt and black pepper
1 cinnamon stick
juice of 1–2 lemons
¾ cup rice, washed and drained
½ cup finely chopped parsley for garnish

Place chicken, giblets, celery, leeks if using, garlic and
water in a pot and bring to a boil. Skim off the top.

Add salt, pepper, cinnamon and the juice of 1 lemon
to the soup broth. Cover and simmer until chicken is
very tender.

Remove bones, leaving only chicken pieces in the
broth. Return to heat, bring to the boil, add the rice and
simmer until rice is cooked.

Adjust seasoning, adding more lemon if necessary.
Garnish with chopped parsley.

Variation When soup is cooked, remove from heat. In a
bowl, beat 3 eggs well with the juice of 1 lemon. Add a
ladleful of the soup to the egg and lemon mixture and
beat it in well. Pour this back into the pot of soup
slowly, beating constantly. Return to very low heat and
cook gently, stirring constantly until it thickens. Do not
allow the soup to boil or the eggs will curdle. Adjust
seasonings, adding more lemon juice if necessary.

Garnish with chopped parsley and serve
immediately.

Stuffed chicken and soup Shourbet djaaj mihshi

Serves 4–6
Cooking time 1–2 hours

1 boiler chicken
2 cups Rice Stuffing for Poultry (see page 55)
1 cup ghee or substitute (see page 19)
3 teaspoons salt
$^1/_2$ teaspoon black pepper
1 cinnamon stick
$^1/_4$ cup rice, washed and drained

Lightly stuff the chicken (including the skin of the neck cavity), allowing for rice expansion, using about 1$^1/_2$ cups stuffing. Sew up the openings with coarse white cotton thread.

Brown the chicken all over in ghee, then place in a large pot. Cover chicken with water and add salt, pepper and cinnamon stick. Bring to a boil.

Skim the top of the broth, turn down the heat, cover the pot and simmer until nearly cooked, about 1 hour. Add the rice and remainder of the stuffing to the broth and continue cooking until the chicken is very tender, about 30 minutes.

Remove the chicken and cinnamon stick from the broth. Remove the cotton, cut the chicken into pieces and keep warm. Skim the fat from the top of the broth and adjust the salt to taste. Serve the broth in individual bowls, and place the chicken and stuffing on a platter in the centre of the table.

Pumpkin soup Shourbet ya'teen

Serves 4–6
Cooking time $^3/_4$ hour plus 1$^1/_2$ hours for Basic Meat Broth

2$^1/_2$ pints (1.25 L) Basic Meat Broth plus meat (see page 43)
2 lb (1 kg) pumpkin, peeled and sliced
$^1/_2$ tablespoon ghee or substitute (see page 19)
1 tablespoon plain flour

Bring the Basic Meat Broth to a boil. Add the pumpkin and cook slowly until tender, about 30 minutes. Remove from heat. Melt ghee in a small saucepan and add the flour, stirring gently until the flour begins to brown. Add a little broth to the flour mixture and stir well.

Transfer the flour mixture to the broth and pumpkin. Purée using a strainer or blender, return to the heat and bring back to a boil. Adjust seasonings.

Serve immediately.

Lentil and spinach soup Adas b'sbaanegh

This recipe requires eight spinach leaves but only a few stalks. Use the remaining stalks for the salad recipe on page 99.

Serves 4–6   **V**   **L**
Cooking time 1 hour

1¹/₂ cups brown or green lentils, prepared and washed (see
   page 15)
7 cups water
³/₄ cup chopped onions
¹/₂ cup olive oil
8 spinach leaves plus a few stalks, chopped finely
2 cloves garlic crushed with 1¹/₂ teaspoons salt
1 celery stalk, finely chopped
¹/₂ cup lemon juice
1 teaspoon cornflour/cornstarch (optional)

Place the lentils in a saucepan with 7 cups of water and bring to a boil. Cover and simmer until tender.

Brown the onions in oil. Add the chopped spinach and the garlic crushed with salt, and mix well. Sauté gently until the spinach becomes soft.

Bring the lentils back to a boil and add the celery and the sautéed mixture. Turn the heat to low and simmer gently for 5 minutes.

For a thin soup, mix in the lemon juice and adjust salt to taste. For a thicker soup, mix the cornflour/cornstarch with the lemon juice before adding it to the cooked soup, then allow soup to simmer for a few minutes longer.

Bur'ghul and lentil soup M'judra humra

Serves 4–6   **V**   **L**
Cooking time 2 hours

1 cup brown or green lentils, prepared and washed (see
   page 15)
5 cups water
2 medium onions, cut into fine rings
¹/₂ cup olive oil
1 cup bur'ghul, washed and drained (see page 14)
1 tablespoon salt

Boil the lentils in the water until soft.

Fry the onions in the oil until very dark brown (practically black). Drain the onions, reserving the oil and set aside.

Add the bur'ghul to the cooked lentils and bring to a boil. While boiling, slowly add the hot oil from the onions. Add salt. Cover and simmer slowly.

When drained, browned onion rings are dry and crisp, crush them into a paste.

Mix the onion paste into the simmering lentil and bur'ghul mixture. Continue to simmer until bur'ghul is soft, about 1¹/₂–2 hours. The soup must be stirred regularly while cooking to prevent it sticking to the bottom, and boiling water may be added if required to keep a thick, creamy consistency. Adjust salt to taste.

Variation Purée the soup and add salt to taste.

Wheat ball and lentil soup Kibbit'healeh

Serves 4–6   **V**   **L**
Cooking time 1 hour

1 cup bur'ghul, washed and drained (see page 14)
1/2 cup plain flour
1/2 tablespoon salt
1/4 teaspoon chilli powder
1/2 cup finely chopped spring onions
1 tablespoon finely chopped mint
1/4 cup finely chopped parsley
1/2 cup brown or green lentils, prepared and washed (see page 15)
4 1/2 cups water
2 large spinach leaves finely chopped
1 small potato, cut in small cubes
1/4 cup lemon juice
1–2 cloves garlic, crushed
1/4 cup olive oil

Mix together the bur'ghul, flour, 1/4 tablespoon salt, chilli powder, spring onions, mint and parsley. Add enough water to make a thick dough. Mould the dough into small balls (about the size of large marbles) and set aside.

Place the lentils in 4 1/2 cups water, bring to a boil and continue boiling for 10 minutes. Add the chopped spinach, potato and remainder of the salt. Turn down heat and simmer until lentils are tender—approx 20–25 minutes. (At this stage the soup should be a medium-thick consistency. If it is too thick, thin it with boiling water).

Bring the soup to a boil and while bubbling add the wheat balls and half the lemon juice. Continue to boil for 5 minutes, add the remainder of the lemon juice, the crushed garlic and the olive oil. Turn down the heat and simmer until the wheat balls are cooked through, about 10 minutes. Adjust salt and lemon to taste.

Serve hot or cold.

Bean and grain soup Makh'loota

Serves 4–6   **V**
Cooking time 1 1/4 hours

1/2 cup chick peas, soaked overnight (see page 14)
1/2 cup red or black beans, soaked overnight (see page 14)
1/2 cup brown or green lentils, prepared and washed (see page 15)
9 cups water
1 tablespoon salt
1/4 cup bur'ghul, washed and drained (see page 14)
1/4 cup rice, washed and drained
1 large onion, finely sliced
1/2 cup olive or nut oil

Drain the soaked chick peas and beans and place in a large saucepan with the lentils, water and salt. Bring to a boil, cover and simmer vigorously for 30 minutes. Add the bur'ghul and rice.

Fry the finely sliced onion in the oil until reddish-brown, then pour both the onions and the very hot oil into the simmering bean and grain mixture.

Cover the mixture and continue to simmer, stirring occasionally, until the rice and bur'ghul are cooked, about 35–40 minutes. Turn down the heat to very low and cook for a further 10 minutes, adding more water if necessary. Adjust salt to taste.

Meatball soup Shourbet el eema

Serves 4–6
Cooking time 3/4 hour plus 1 1/2 hours for Basic Meat
Broth

1 full cup ground meat
1 teaspoon salt
1/4 teaspoon pepper
1/4 teaspoon mixed spices (see page 15)
3 tablespoons ghee or substitute (see page 19)
2 1/2 pints (1.25 L) Basic Meat Broth plus meat (see page 43)
1/2 cup tomato juice or 1 tablespoon tomato paste mixed
with 1/2 cup water
1/4 cup rice, washed and drained
1/4 cup chopped parsley
1/4 teaspoon ground cinnamon

Mix ground meat with salt, pepper and mixed spices.
Shape into balls the size of marbles. Brown in hot
ghee.

Bring the broth to a boil, add the meatballs, tomato
juice and rice and simmer until the meatballs are
cooked through, about 20–30 minutes.

Add parsley and cinnamon just before serving.
Adjust seasonings to taste.

Basic meat broth

Makes 3 pints (1.5 L)
Cooking time 1 1/2–2 hours

2 lb (1 kg) soup meat, cubed
several soup bones, cracked
3 tablespoons ghee or substitute (see page 19)
2 1/2 pints (1.25 L) water
1/2 tablespoon salt

In a large saucepan lightly brown the meat and bones
in the ghee, then drain. Pour in the water, add the salt
and bring to a boil. Skim fat off the top.

Cover saucepan, turn down heat and simmer,
adding more water if necessary. Cook until meat is
tender enough to fall off the bones, about 1 1/2–2 hours.

fish

The waters off the coast of Lebanon offer a wealth of seafood, so it is not surprising that fish forms the basis of many popular recipes. It is generally cooked whole and served with a special spicy rice (see page 46) or fried potatoes and Tahini Sauce or Pine Nut Sauce (see page 18).

To prepare fish for cooking, clean and scale the fish, leaving on the head but removing the eyes. Salt inside and out, then refrigerate for several hours. Allow it to return to room temperature before cooking.

Lebanese fish dishes are always garnished with wedges of lemon and small pieces of Lebanese bread fried in the same oil as the fish. Accompaniments include small pieces of fried vegetables such as cauliflower, zucchini and eggplant, and dips such as Hoummus b'Tahini (see page 29) and Baba Ghannouj (see page 26).

Fried fish Sumak mi'li

Serves 4
Cooking time 10–15 minutes

4 small whole fish or 1 large fish cut into pieces
flour
olive or nut oil

Prepare fish as directed opposite.
Dredge fish in flour and deep-fry or shallow-fry in oil until golden brown and cooked through. Remove and let stand to drain off excess oil.

Serve accompanied by Tahini Sauce or Pine Nut Sauce (see page 18), small pieces of fried cauliflower, and Lebanese bread fried in the oil in which the fish was cooked.

Fish stew Yakh'nit sumak

Serves 5
Cooking time 30 minutes

1 fish, about 2 lb (1 kg)
2 cups olive oil
2 medium onions, sliced
salt
$^1/_4$ teaspoon powdered saffron
$^1/_2$ cup lemon juice

Prepare the fish as directed opposite.
Brown fish lightly in olive oil—do not cook through. Remove fish and place in saucepan.
Brown the onions in the same oil and drain well.
Mix the onions, salt, saffron and lemon juice, and add to the fish with enough water to cover. Simmer gently until the fish is very tender.
When the fish is cooked, lift it out and remove the flesh from the bones. Lay the fish fillets on a platter.
Season the sauce and pour over the fish. Serve with Spicy Rice for Fish (see page 46).

Spicy rice for fish Ruz lissumak

Serves 4–6
Cooking time 30 minutes

¹/₄ cup olive or nut oil
¹/₂ cup pine nuts
1 cup sliced onions
2 cups rice, washed and drained
1 teaspoon salt
3¹/₂ cups boiling water
¹/₄ teaspoon powdered saffron

Heat the oil in a saucepan and lightly fry the pine nuts. Remove and set aside.

Lightly brown the onions in the same oil. Add the rice and salt, and sauté for a few minutes.

Pour in the boiling water and saffron. Allow to bubble for a few seconds, cover tightly and turn down to a low simmer. Cook until all the water is absorbed and the rice is tender, about 20 minutes.

To serve, turn out rice onto a platter, sprinkle with the pine nuts and garnish with fish pieces. Alternatively, serve as an accompaniment to a fish dish.

For added fish flavour, oil left over from frying fish may be used in this recipe.

Fish and rice stew Seeyadeeyeh

Serves 4–6
Cooking time 1¹/₂ hours

1 fish, about 4 lb (2 kg)
¹/₂ cup pine nuts
1¹/₄ cups olive or nut oil
2 medium onions, cut into rings
7¹/₂ cups water
2¹/₂ teaspoons salt
2¹/₂ cups rice, washed and drained
¹/₂ teaspoon ground cumin
¹/₄ cup lemon juice
parsley sprigs for garnish

Prepare the fish as directed on page 44.

Lightly brown the pine nuts in ¹/₄ cup of the oil, remove, drain and set aside. Add the remaining oil and fry the onions until very dark brown (but not burnt). Remove the onions and allow to drain.

Place the water in a large saucepan and bring to a boil. Add the onions and continue boiling until soft. Remove the onions from the saucepan and purée through a sieve or strainer back into the boiling water.

Place the fish in the boiling water and add the salt. Simmer until cooked, about 40 minutes.

Remove the fish from the broth, fillet and keep warm.

Place 5 cups of the broth and the oil in which the onions were fried in another saucepan, bring to a boil and add the rice and cumin. Cover and simmer gently until rice is cooked and fluid is absorbed, about 20 minutes.

Make a sauce with 2 cups of the broth and the lemon juice. Place the fish on a large platter with the rice. Garnish with parsley and pine nuts and serve accompanied by the sauce.

Baked fish Sumki makh'boozeh

Serves 4–6
Cooking time 40 minutes

1 large whole fish, about 5 lb (2.5 kg)
1/2 cup olive or nut oil
2 lemons cut into round slices
chopped parsley for garnish

Prepare fish as directed on page 44.

Rub fish well with olive or nut oil. Place on a layer of lemon slices in a baking dish.

Cook in a preheated moderate oven for 30 minutes, turn over and continue cooking for a further 10 minutes or until flesh is white.

Serve garnished with chopped parsley and accompanied by Tahini Sauce or Pine Nut Sauce (see page 18).

Baked fish in tahini sauce Sumki b'tahini

Serves 2
Cooking time about 40 minutes

1 whole fish, about 2 lb (1 kg)
1/2 cup olive or nut oil
1 medium onion, chopped
1 cup Tahini Sauce without parsley (see page 18)
1/4 cup finely chopped parsley and wedges of lemon for
    garnish

Prepare fish as directed on page 44.

Rub the fish with half the oil and bake in a preheated moderate oven until cooked. The flesh should be white and flake apart easily when prodded with a fork.

Fry onion lightly in the remainder of the oil, until transparent. Drain. Mix the onion into the Tahini Sauce, pour over the baked fish and bake for a further 10 minutes in a low oven.

Garnish with chopped parsley and wedges of lemon. Serve hot with Spicy Rice for Fish (see page 46) or cold with salads.

Baked peppered fish Sumki har'rah

Serves 4
Cooking time 45 minutes

1 whole fish, about 4–5 lb (2–2.5 kg)
3/4 cup olive or nut oil
2 medium onions, finely chopped
1 large green pepper, finely chopped
1/2 hot pepper, finely chopped (optional)
1/2 teaspoon freshly ground black pepper
3/4 cup walnut pieces, finely crushed
1 cup finely chopped parsley
2 cups Tahini Sauce (see page 18)
1 lemon, cut into thick slices, for garnish

Prepare the fish as directed on page 44.

Pour 1/4 cup of the oil into a shallow baking dish. Place the fish in the dish, pour another 1/4 cup of oil over it and leave at room temperature for 15 minutes.

Gently heat the remaining oil in a large, heavy frying pan. Add the onions and cook for about 10 minutes, stirring frequently, until they are soft and golden brown. Stir in the green pepper, hot pepper if using, black pepper and walnuts and cook for 2–3 minutes until the peppers are soft. Turn off the heat and add 1/2 cup parsley.

Without removing fish from the baking dish, fill with the walnut mixture. Close the opening with small skewers and criss-cross kitchen string around them to secure.

Bake the fish in the centre of a prerheated moderate oven, 350°F (180°C/Gas 4), basting it every 15 minutes until cooked (when it feels firm to touch or flakes easily when prodded with a fork), about 40–50 minutes.

Remove skewers and spread fish evenly with Tahini Sauce. Sprinkle with the remainder of the parsley and garnish with lemon slices. Serve hot or cold.

Variation For Baked Walnut Fish (Sumki b'Jose), omit one of the onions, the hot pepper and the Tahini Sauce. You may also like to reduce the amount of black pepper and increase the walnuts.

poultry

Originally the Lebanese raised chickens for eggs rather than meat, and only older birds were butchered. To improve the flavour of the "tough old hen" and keep it moist, they developed recipes with tasty stuffings, spices and herbs—ideal for enhancing the taste of modern mass-produced chickens. Roasted pigeons and larks are a great delicacy in Lebanon, however as these birds are protected in some Western countries the recipes have been withheld.

Poultry for Lebanese dishes is always prepared by washing and drying well, then rubbing with salt inside and out. Unless otherwise stated poultry is cooked whole, but it is always served in pieces on a large platter.

Barbecued garlic chicken Djaaj mishwi

Serves 2
Cooking time about 20 minutes

1 small tender chicken
4 cloves garlic, crushed
1 teaspoon salt
juice of 1/2 lemon
1/2 cup olive oil

Cut the chicken in half or quarters.

Mix remaining ingredients together to make a marinade. Reserve 1/4 cup of this marinade and rub the remainder into the chicken. Marinate for 2–4 hours.

Barbecue or grill the chicken, basting it frequently with the reserved marinade. Serve hot, accompanied by Garlic Sauce (see page 19) and salads.

Chicken on skewers Djaaj mishwi b'ssaineeyeh

Serves 2–4
Cooking time 10–15 minutes

2 small chickens
1 cup finely grated onion
6 cloves garlic, crushed
1 cup lemon juice
3 tablespoons olive oil
salt

Bone chickens and cut meat into cubes suitable for skewering. Blend the onion and garlic into the lemon juice and olive oil. Add salt and marinate the chicken pieces in this mixture for 2–4 hours, turning occasionally.

Thread chicken pieces closely together on skewers. Barbecue for 10–15 minutes, preferable over charcoal.

Serve with Garlic Sauce (see page 19), Hoummus b'Tahini (see page 29) or Baba Ghannouj (see page 26), and Tabbouleh (see page 96).

Chicken with chick peas and rice
Djaaj b'hoummus ou ruz

The ideal pasta for this recipe is the very small Risone No. 63, which resembles brown rice. It is available at continental delicatessens and some supermarkets. Broken-up vermicelli is a suitable substitute.

Serves 4–6
Cooking time 1½ hours

1 large chicken
1 cup ghee or substitute (see page 19)
12 cups water
2 medium onions, finely chopped
1 clove garlic, crushed
1 cinnamon stick
4 teaspoons salt
³/4 cup chick peas, soaked overnight (see page 14)
½ cup slivered almonds
1 lb (500 g) coarsely ground meat
½ teaspoon ground cinnamon
½ teaspoon black pepper
³/4 cup Risone Pasta No. 63 or broken up vermicelli
1 cup rice, washed and drained

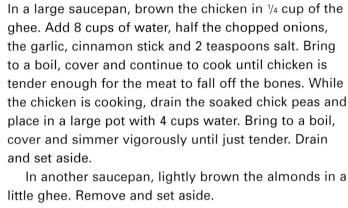

In a large saucepan, brown the chicken in ¼ cup of the ghee. Add 8 cups of water, half the chopped onions, the garlic, cinnamon stick and 2 teaspoons salt. Bring to a boil, cover and continue to cook until chicken is tender enough for the meat to fall off the bones. While the chicken is cooking, drain the soaked chick peas and place in a large pot with 4 cups water. Bring to a boil, cover and simmer vigorously until just tender. Drain and set aside.

In another saucepan, lightly brown the almonds in a little ghee. Remove and set aside.

Add ¼ cup of the ghee to the saucepan and heat. Fry the meat in the ghee, stirring occasionally, until brown all over. Turn down heat to simmer and cook until nearly tender, about 15 minutes.

Stir in the cinnamon, black pepper and the remainder of the onions and salt, and continue to cook for a further 25 minutes. Remove from saucepan and set aside.

Place the remaining ½ cup of ghee in the same saucepan and sauté the pasta or vermicelli until golden brown. Add the rice and sauté for a few more minutes.

Pour 5 cups of the boiling broth from the cooked chicken over the rice (make up quantity with water if necessary). Bring to a boil and add the cooked meat and onion mixture and the cooked chick peas. Stir well, cover, turn down heat to simmer and cook until the rice is tender and the liquid is absorbed, about 20 minutes. Turn off heat and let stand for 10 minutes.

Serve the chick pea and rice mixture on a platter, garnished with the almonds and chicken pieces.

Chicken with onions Djaaj b'bassal

Serves 4–6
Cooking time 1–1½ hours

½ cup ghee or substitute (see page 19)
6 very small onions, peeled and left whole
1 large tender chicken
1 tablespoon flour
6 cups boiling water
2 teaspoons salt
½ teaspoon black pepper
1 teaspoon mixed spices (see page 15)
½ cup lemon juice

Heat the ghee in a large frying pan, add the onions and chicken and cook until brown. Remove the onions and set aside, and transfer the chicken to a large pot.

Drain the ghee from the frying pan, leaving just enough to brown the flour.

Brown the flour, stir in the boiling water and simmer for a few minutes. When the mixture is smooth pour it over the chicken. Add salt, pepper and spices. Cover and simmer on stovetop or place in a preheated 325°F (170°C/Gas 3) oven and cook as a casserole.

Add the fried onions halfway through cooking time, after about 30–45 minutes.

Stir in the lemon juice just before serving.

To serve, remove the onions and place them on a serving platter. Arrange the chicken pieces over the onions and pour some of the chicken juice over the top. Accompany with Rice Pilaf (see page 23).

Stuffed turkey Habash mihshi

Serves 8–10
Cooking time about 20 minutes for each 1 lb (500 g) of turkey

1 turkey, apbout 13–17 lb (6–8 kg)
4 cups Rice Stuffing for Poultry (see page 55)
water
2 tablespoons salt
2 cups yoghurt or 1 cup ghee (see page 19)

Remove the neck bone and stuff the turkey, including the neck skin, with the rice stuffing. Sew up the opening with coarse white thread.

Place the turkey in a large pot with enough water to barely cover. Add the salt, bring to a boil and skim. Cover and simmer gently until tender.

When cooked, remove the turkey from the pot and place in a roasting tray. Coat with yoghurt or ghee and brown in a preheated hot oven. Remove cotton thread.

Slice the turkey and serve on a platter together with stuffing.

Stuffed roast chicken Djaaj mihshi

Serves 4
Cooking time 1³/₄ hours

1 roasting chicken
2 cups Rice Stuffing for Poultry (see opposite)
¹/₂ cup ghee or substitute (see page 19)
1 cup water
¹/₂ teaspoon salt
1 tablespoon cornflour/cornstarch mixed to a paste with a
little water

Prepare and stuff the chicken with rice stuffing as in the recipe for Stuffed Chicken and Soup (see page 39).

Rub stuffed chicken with ghee, wrap in aluminium foil and bake in a preheated moderate oven, 350–400°F (180–200°C/Gas 4–6) for 1¹/₄ hours. Remove foil and continue to bake until tender and browned.

Make a gravy by heating the water, salt and ¹/₂ cup of the juice from the cooked chicken in a small saucepan. Stir in the cornflour/cornstarch paste just before the mixture comes to a boil and continue stirring until it thickens.

Cut the chicken into pieces and serve on a platter with the stuffing, accompanied by the gravy.

Rice stuffing for poultry Hashwit djaaj b'ruz

Makes 4 cups
Cooking time 25 minutes

3 tablespoons ghee or substitute
³/₄ cup pine nuts
2 medium onions, finely chopped
1 lb (500 g) meat, coarsely ground or finely chopped
2 teaspoons salt
¹/₄ teaspoon pepper
¹/₂ teaspoon mixed spices (see page 15)
¹/₄ teaspoon ground cinnamon
1¹/₄ cups cooked rice

Heat the ghee in a pan and lightly brown the pine nuts. Remove and set aside.

Add the meat to the ghee and fry for a few minutes until the raw look disappears. Before the meat browns, mix in the chopped onions, salt, pepper, mixed spices and cinnamon. Cover, turn down to medium heat and continue to cook until meat is very tender and the juices are absorbed, about 20–25 minutes.

Remove from heat, mix in the pine nuts then mix into rice. Mix well.

kibbi

Kibbi is the national dish of Lebanon. Basically a mixture of ground meat and bur'ghul (a crushed wheat, see page 14), it is extremely nourishing, yet economical, and can be used in a variety of ways—raw, baked, stuffed or with sauces.

The ideal meat for kibbi is a leg of mutton. Young lamb is unsuitable for most dishes as the meat is too tender and does not bind together well, however it may be used for Kibbi Nayye (kibbi eaten raw). As a last resort, ground lean topside beef may be substituted for mutton.

Nowadays in Lebanon the meat for kibbi can be bought already prepared from the butcher, but until recently the preparation was a time-consuming ritual. The pounding of the meat in a stone or metal mortar (jorn) with a heavy pestle (madaqqa) was a long and tedious procedure. Today a fine bladed electric mincer or food processor is used.

We have included the full method of preparing kibbi meat (in the recipe for the Basic Kibbi Mixture), however if you want to save time you may find a Lebanese butcher from whom kibbi meat can be bought already prepared and ground. Alternatively, your local butcher might prepare the mutton leg for you if you give enough notice.

Basic kibbi mixture

This recipe forms the basis of all kibbi dishes. As it is impossible to estimate exactly how much ground meat you will get from a leg of mutton, we have given only approximate measures for both it and the bur'ghul.

When measuring these basic ingredients be sure to keep the proportions at 1^1/$_2$ cups of bur'ghul to every 1 lb (500 g) of ground meat. It is essential to keep the mixture cold while kneading and grinding.

Makes 5 lb (2.5 kg)—enough to make 2–4 varieties of kibbi for 4–6 people

about 4^1/$_2$ cups bur'ghul (see page 14)
1 leg of mutton to make about 3 lb (1.5 kg) ground meat
3 medium onions
1 red pepper
1 tablespoon salt or to taste
1 tablespoon freshly ground black pepper
1 teaspoon mixed spices (see page 15)
^{1}/$_2$ teaspoon ground cinnamon
iced water or ice

Wash the bur'ghul in cold water and drain well by taking handfuls and squeezing out the water. (It is a good idea to wash and drain bur'ghul a few hours before making up this recipe. Keep it in the refrigerator until required.)

With a sharp knife remove the meat from the bone, then remove all the fat and gristle from the meat. Grind the lean meat twice through the fine blade of the mincer.

Grind the onions and red pepper and knead them into the meat together with the salt, pepper, mixed spices and cinnamon. (For a spicier flavour, you may substitute a chilli pepper for the red pepper as a variation.) Knead the bur'ghul into the meat mixture, occasionally adding 1 tablespoon of iced water or a small piece of ice to keep the mixture smooth and cold.

Put the kneaded mixture through the fine blade of the mincer twice. For the best results, refrigerate in a covered container for 6–12 hours then knead again for a few minutes before cooking.

If you do not have a mincer: Buy finely ground meat and knead all ingredients well for 30 minutes, constantly adding small amounts of iced water to keep the mixture cool and smooth. Refrigerate for a few hours and knead well again for about 15 minutes before cooking.

Kibbi eaten raw Kibbi nayye

When kibbi is to be eaten raw, the proportion of bur'ghul to meat is generally reduced to 1 cup bur'ghul to every 1 lb (500 g) of ground meat, however the Basic Kibbi Mixture (see opposite) is a satisfactory alternative. Kibbi Nayye should always be eaten the same day—use any leftovers for cooked kibbi dishes.

Serves 6–8

2 lb (1 kg) Basic Kibbi Mixture

Make kibbi mixture as for basic recipe (see opposite).

Mould the mixture into oval shapes half the size of a small saucer, arrange on a serving platter and garnish with fresh mint.

This dish is generally served with a small jug of olive oil for pouring and is accompanied by a peeled and quartered raw onion, Hot Pepper and Onion Paste (see below) or Meat and Nut Filling (see page 22), and fresh bread. It may also be eaten plain or spread thickly on a slice of bread as an open sandwich.

Hot pepper and onion paste Titbeeleh

This paste is generally eaten with Kibbi Nayye.

Makes ½ cup **V** **L**

1 medium onion
1 small hot red pepper
salt

Grind or blend all the ingredients together into a paste.

Baked kibbi in oil Kibbi b'zait

1 cup olive oil or substitute oil
2 lb (1 kg) Basic Kibbi Mixture (see opposite)

Grease a shallow-edged baking dish, about 12 in x 10 in (30 cm x 25 cm) in size, with olive oil.

Place the kibbe mixture in the baking dish, pat and smooth down with wet hands until the tray is evenly covered with the mixture ½ in (1.5 cm) thick. Make deep horizontal or diagonal lines to form square or diamond shapes in the mixture so the oil can penetrate (see picture below).

Cover the mixture with a thick film of oil and bake on the centre shelf of a perheated oven at 450°F (230°C/Gas 8) for about 20 minutes, then move to the top shelf for 10 minutes to brown the top.

This kibbi is delicious eaten hot or cold, wrapped in bread as a snack or accompanied by yoghurt and a fresh green salad.

Baked stuffed kibbi loaf Kibbi b'tab'etain

Serves 6–8
Cooking time 1–1¼ hours

1 cup ghee or substitute (see page 19)
4 lb (2 kg) Basic Kibbi Mixture (see page 36)
3 cups Meat and Nut Filling (see page 22)

With a little of the ghee, thoroughly grease a 12-in (30-cm) square baking tray.

With wet hands smooth half the kibbi mixture into the tray, covering the bottom completely to ½ in (1.5 cm) thick.

Spread the filling evenly over the kibbi on the tray, then cover the filling with the remainder of the kibbi mixture to the same ½-in (1.5-cm) thickness. Cut deep horizontal or diagonal lines through both layers of the kibbi to form square or diamond shapes so the ghee can penetrate.

Dot the remainder of the ghee on top of the kibbi in the tray and place in a preheated moderate oven, 350–400°F (180–200°C/Gas 4–6), until golden brown on top, about 1–1¼ hours.

Serve hot or cold with stews, yoghurt or salads.

Kibbi shells

Kibbiyet and Or'rus are shells moulded from the Basic Kibbi Mixture. Kibbiyet are long oval-shaped shells, filled or left hollow, which are baked or deep fried. Or'rus are pie-shaped shells, filled with hot shortening or meat filling, which are grilled.

Oval kibbi shells Kibbiyet

Makes 6–10 kibbiyet
Cooking time 10–15 minutes

1 lb (500 g) Basic Kibbi Mixture (see page 56)
Meat and Nut Filling (see page 22) (optional)
olive or nut oil, for frying, or ½ cup ghee or substitute (see page 19) for baking

With wet hands, mould the kibbi mixture into balls a little larger than then size of a golf ball.

Take one kibbi ball in your left hand and with the index finger of your right hand make a hole in it. Work the finger around the hole until a long thin shell is formed. The shell should be thin and smooth. Keep hands wet during the procedure and repair breaks in the shell with wet fingers. Repeat with remaining balls.

Fill each shell with 2 teaspoons of Meat and Nut Filling or leave empty. Close the openings with wet fingers and smooth the shells into oval shapes or pat them back into round shapes.

Deep-fry the shells in oil or bake them in ghee in an oven tray.

Pie-shaped kibbi shells Or'rus

Makes 4–6 or'rus
Cooking time 15–20 minutes

1 lb (500 g) Basic Kibbi Mixture (see page 56)
1¹/₂–2 cups Meat and Nut Filling (see page 22), or 1 cup solid
  butter, margarine or ground mutton fat
salt

With wet hands, mould some of the kibbi mixture into a dish shape, about the size of a small saucer, 3 in (8 cm) in diameter. Lay the shell upside-down over a small inverted soup bowl and make an identical shell.

Fill the second shell with Meat and Nut Filling or solid butter, margarine or ground mutton fat.

Place the first shell over the second shell to form a pie shape. With wet hands securely seal the rims of both shells together.

Repeat the above procedure until all the kibbi has been used.

Rub the top of each Or'rus with slightly salted water. Place under a very hot grill and cook until browned on top, then turn over and brown yhe underside.

Kibbi balls in yoghurt Lubb'neehey

When making this dish it is important to remember never to cover the yoghurt while cooking and always to stir it in the one direction to prevent curdling.

Serves 8
Cooking time 1 hour

1 cup Basic Kibbi Mixture (see page 56)
¹/₂ cup rice, washed and drained
2 cups water
3 cups yoghurt
1 egg white
1 teaspoon salt
lemon juice to taste (optional)

With wet hands, mould the kibbi mixture into small hollow balls about the size and shape of a small egg (see Kibbiyet directions on this page 58).

Place the rice and water in a saucepan and bring quickly to a boil. Lower heat to simmer, cover and cook until rice is nearly tender and most of the water is absorbed.

Beat together the yoghurt, egg white and salt. Add this mixture to the simmering rice and beat with egg beater. The mixture should have the consistency of thick soup. Add more water if necessary.

Bring the mixture back to a boil, stirring occasionally to prevent it sticking to the bottom of the pan. Stir in the kibbi balls gently and continue to boil for 5 minutes; then lower heat and simmer for a further 5 minutes. Turn off the heat and cover saucepan. Let stand for 5 minutes before serving. If a more tart flavour is required, add lemon juice to taste before serving.

Kibbi balls and chick peas in tahini
Kibbi arnabeeyeh

Serves 6–8
Cooking time 1½ hours

1 lb (500 g) Basic Kibbi Mixture (see page 56)
2 large onions, chopped in large pieces
½ cup ghee or substitute (see page 19)
1 lb (500 g) meat and bones for broth (preferably mutton)
water
1½ cups chick peas, soaked overnight (see page 14)
1½ cups tahini (see page 16)
½ cup lemon juice

With wet hands, mould the kibbi mixture into small balls and place aside.

Brown the onions in the ghee and drain.

Cover the meat and bones with water and bring to a boil; skim fat from the top of the water. Add the drained, soaked chick peas and the browned onions. Simmer mixture for 1½ hours, then remove the meat from the broth to prevent overcooking.

Bring the broth to a boil. Mix the tahini well with the lemon juice and pour into the boiling broth. Add the kibbi balls and continue to boil for 10 minutes.

Return meat to the broth, turn down heat and simmer slowly until the oil from the tahini floats to the top. Serve hot, accompanied by a bowl of Rice Pilaf (see page 23).

Kibbi balls with meat pies and yoghurt
Kibbi shishbarak

Serves 6–8
Cooking time 1 hour 5 minutes

1 lb (500 g) Basic Kibbi Mixture (see page 56)
1½ cups plain flour
½ cup water
1 cup Meat and Nut Filling (see page 22)
2½ pints (1.25 L) Cooked Yoghurt (see page 21)

With wet hands, mould the kibbi mixture into small balls about half the size of an egg.

Make the flour and water into a simple dough and roll out thinly. Using a biscuit cutter, cut into circles about 1½ in (4 cm) in diameter.

Place 1 teaspoon of the Meat and Nut Filling on one side of each dough circle, then fold the other side of the circle over the top, pressing the edges together to form a crescent-shaped pie (shishbarak).

Arrange the pies on a greased baking sheet and place them in a preheated moderate oven long enough only to dry out the dough. Alternatively they can be dried by exposing to the air.

Prepare the yoghurt as directed on page 21, and while it is simmering add the kibbi balls. After 10 minutes add the little pies and continue to simmer for a further 10–15 minutes.

Although not true kibbi dishes, the following fish and Lenten recipes are based on the traditional Baked Meat Kibbi meat bake, Kibbi b'Zait.

Fish kibbi Kibbit sumak

Serves 6–8
Cooking time 35 minutes

3 lb (1.5 kg) jewfish or mackerel fillets
2 medium onions, finely ground
3 teaspoons salt
1 teaspoon white pepper
2 teaspoons ground coriander
2 tablespoons grated orange peel
1 cup finely chopped parsley
4 cups bur'ghul, washed and drained (see page 14)
cooked rice, for binding
¼ cup olive or nut oil
3 medium onions, cut into rings
½ cup pine nuts
¼ teaspoon powdered saffron

Skin the fish fillets and cut into small pieces. Finely grind them in a mincer.

Add the ground onions, salt, pepper, coriander, grated orange peel and chopped parsley. Mix well.

Gradually knead in the bur'ghul, adding a little rice during the process to help bind the mixture.

Put the mixture through the mincer.

Heat the oil in a large baking dish, about 14 in x 12 in (35 cm x 30 cm) in size, and lightly sauté the onion rings and pine nuts. Remove the dish from the heat, spread the onions and nuts evenly over the bottom and sprinkle with saffron. Spread a layer of the kibbi mixture evenly over the onions to a thickness of about ½ in (1.25 cm). Cut through as in meat kibbi (see page 57).

Bake in a preheated hot oven, 425°F (220°C/Gas 7), until golden brown, about 30 minutes.

Serve hot with Spicy Rice for Fish (see page 46) or cold with salads.

Potato and wheat loaf Kibbit batata

Serves 8   V   L
Cooking time 45–50 minutes

1½ lb (750 g) potatoes
2 large onions, ground or grated
1½ tablespoons salt
½ teaspoon black pepper
1 teaspoon ground cinnamon
1½ cups bur'ghul (see page 14)
1 cup plain flour
1 cup finely chopped parsley
¼ cup finely chopped mint
1½ cups olive or nut oil

Boil the potatoes in their jackets, then peel and pound to a paste like consistency with the ground or grated onion, salt, pepper and ground cinnamon. Knead in the bur'ghul, then the flour. Add the parsley and mint and knead again.

Bake in a baking dish with oil exactly as for Kibbi b'Zait (see page 57).

Serve cold, either by itself or with salad or bread.

meat

In the past, meat was not always plentiful or of good quality. To overcome these problems it was either ground or cut into small pieces and cooked with cereals and vegetables to absorb the nutrients and flavour of the juices and to make the meat go further. Although good quality meat is now readily available in Lebanon, the popularity of the traditional meat recipes has not waned. They are generally made with lamb or mutton, but beef is a satisfactory substitute.

Meat on skewers Lahem mishwi

Serves 4–6
Cooking time 10–15 minutes

2 lb (1 kg) tender lamb (preferably from the leg) or tender beef
$1/2$ cup olive oil or substitute
4 cloves crushed garlic
1 teaspoon mixed spices (see page 15)
salt and black pepper
4 onions, quartered and split
2 green peppers, cut into 1-in (2.5-cm) squares

Cut the meat into 1-in (2.5-cm) cubes, leaving a little fat on some pieces. Place the cubes in a bowl and mix in the oil, garlic, spices, salt and pepper. Refrigerate for 1–2 hours, but remove from refrigerator 1 hour before cooking.

Thread the meat, onion and green pepper pieces onto the skewers alternately. Barbecue or grill them, basting occasionally with the oil and garlic mixture left in the bowl. (If barbecuing, a handful of herbs is often thrown over the fire to give added aroma.)

As soon as the meat is cooked, wrap an open piece of Lebanese bread around the meat to catch the juices and serve accompanied by Tahini Sauce (see page 18) and Tabbouleh (see page 96) or other salads.

Variation The skewered meat and vegetables may be cooked plain, without oil or garlic.

Basic kafta mixture

Kafta mixture is basically finely ground meat, but unlike kibbi it is not made up entirely of lean meat. Kafta may be made from either lamb or beef. Ordinary hamburger ground meat is also quite satisfactory.

Makes 2 lb (1 kg)

2 lb (1 kg) finely ground beef, lamb or hamburger meat
1 cup finely chopped parsley
1 teaspoon mixed spices (see page 15)
1 cup finely chopped or ground onions
3 teaspoons salt
1/2 teaspoon black pepper
iced water

Mix all the ingredients except water in a large bowl and knead well.

Place the mixture through the fine blade of a grinder twice or alternatively knead well for a further 20 minutes, occasionally adding small quantities of iced water.

Kafta on skewers Kafta mishweeyeh b'sseekh

Serves 4–6
Cooking time 10–15 minutes

2 lb (1 kg) Basic Kafta Mixture (see above)

With wet fingers, mould the kafta mixture into meat balls slightly larger than an egg. Thread a skewer through each meat ball and mould the meat into a finger shape along the skewers.

Gently barbecue or grill the meat, making sure not to overcook as it will dry out.

When cooked, remove the meat from the skewers using open pieces of Lebanese bread, which are then left around the meat to make juicy sandwiches. The sandwiches are usually accompanied by Hoummus b'Tahini (see page 29). If preferred, the kafta may be served without bread but accompanied by a salad.

Kafta meat loaf Kafta b'ssaineeyeh

Serves 4–6
Cooking time 40 minutes

2 lb (1 kg) Basic Kafta Mixture (see left)
3 tablespoons tomato paste
1 cup water

Spread the kafta mixture evenly over a large baking tray, about 12 in x 10 in (30 cm x 25 cm) in size, so that it is 1 in (2.5 cm) thick. Bake in a moderate oven until lightly browned, about 10 minutes.

Mix the tomato paste with the water, pour over the meat in the tray and continue baking until half the juice is absorbed into the meat, about 20 minutes.

Remove the tray from the oven, place on a hotplate and keep at moderate heat until most of the juice is absorbed into the meat, about 10 minutes.

Cut into squares and serve hot with mashed potatoes and cooked vegetables.

Fried meat patties Mi'leeyeh

Serves 4–6
Cooking time 15–20 minutes

1 egg white
2 lb (1 kg) Basic Kafta Mixture (see 67)
flour
olive or nut oil

Mix the unbeaten egg white into the kafta mixture.
Mould the mixture into little patties. Dip the patties in
flour and pan-fry in hot oil.

Serve with potato chips and salad or sautéed
vegetables. Hoummus b'Tahini (see page 29) can be
used as a sauce.

Meatballs and pine nuts in tomato sauce Dawood baasha

Serves 6
Cooking time 40 minutes

1 lb (500 g) Basic Kafta Mixture (see page 67), omitting
parsley
1 cup pine nuts
1/2 cup olive or nut oil
2 large onions, chopped
4 medium tomatoes, peeled
2 tablespoons tomato paste blended with 1 cup water
1/2 teaspoon mixed spices (see page 15)
salt and black pepper
juice of half a lemon

Mould the kafta mixture into balls about half the size of
an egg.

In a saucepan, lightly brown the pine nuts in oil,
remove and set aside. Fry the onions in the same oil
until golden brown, remove and set aside. Brown the
meat balls and set aside.

Place the peeled tomatoes and tomato paste
blended with water in the pan and bring to a boil. Add
the mixed spices, salt and pepper, lemon juice, onions
and meat balls. Simmer for 20 minutes, adding a little
more water if required. Add the pine nuts just before
serving.

Serve with Rice Pilaf (see page 23).

Bur'ghul and meat Bur'ghul b'lahem

This dish is equally delicious when cooked with chicken instead of meat.

Serves 4–6
Cooking time 2 hours 50 minutes

2 cups bur'ghul (see page 14)
3 medium onions, finely chopped
1 cup ghee or substitute (see page 19)
1¹/₂ lb (750 g) lean stewing meat, cubed
3 teaspoons salt
¹/₄ teaspoon black pepper
1 teaspoon mixed spices (see page 15)
3 tomatoes, peeled
4 tablespoons tomato paste

Wash and drain the bur'ghul then squeeze out excess water with cupped hands. Set aside for at least 30 minutes.

In a frying pan, fry the onions in half the ghee until soft, add the meat and fry for a few minutes until lightly browned. Season with salt, pepper and spices.

Place the meat and onions in a casserole dish. Add the peeled tomatoes, tomato paste and enough water to cover the meat. Cover and bake in a preheated moderate oven until meat is tender, about 2 hours.

When cooked, drain the sauce from the meat and put 3 cups back into the casserole dish. Bring to a boil.

Add the remaining ghee to the frying pan and gently fry the bur'ghul for 10 minutes, stirring constantly.

Place the bur'ghul in the casserole dish, spreading it evenly over the boiling meat and sauce. Cover and bake in a moderate oven for 30 minutes. It is cooked when the liquid is absorbed and the bur'ghul is moist and fluffy. If the liquid is absorbed before the bur'ghul is cooked, add a little more boiling sauce or water and return to the oven.

Lentils with meat M'judra b'lahem

Serves 4–6
Cooking time 1 hour

1 lb (500 g) coarsely ground meat, preferably mutton or lamb
1 tablespoon ghee or substitute (see page 19)
1 medium onion, finely chopped
1 cup brown lentils, prepared and washed (see page 15)
5 cups water
1 cup rice, washed and drained
1¹/₂ teaspoons salt
¹/₄ teaspoon black pepper

Lightly brown the meat in the hot ghee, add the onion and cook until transparent, about 10 minutes.

Boil the lentils in the water until tender. Drain the water from the lentils and put 2 cups back into the saucepan. If necessary add more water to make up the quantity.

Bring the lentils back to a boil. Stir in the rice, meat and onions, salt and pepper. Allow the mixture to bubble for a few seconds, turn down to simmer, cover tightly and cook until all the water is absorbed, about 15 minutes.

Adjust salt and pepper to taste.

Baked macaroni with meat
Ma'karoni b'ssaneeyeh

Serves 6
Cooking time 1 hour

12 oz (375 g) macaroni pasta
2 large onions, finely chopped
$1/4$ cup ghee or substitute (see page 19)
1 lb (500 g) coarsely ground meat
2 teaspoons salt
$1/2$ teaspoon pepper
$1/2$ teaspoon mixed spices (see page 15)
$1/4$ teaspoon ground cinnamon
1 tablespoon vinegar
4 tablespoons tomato paste
1 cup tomato juice or canned tomato soup
$1/2$ cup water
4 eggs (optional)
$1/2$ cup grated cheese

Cook the macaroni in boiling salted water until tender. Drain, rinse in cold water, drain again and set aside.

Sauté the onions in the ghee, add the meat and cook until brown all over, about 10 minutes. Add the salt, pepper, mixed spices and cinnamon, then stir in the vinegar, tomato paste, tomato juice or soup and the water. Cover and simmer gently until meat is tender, 30–35 minutes.

Spread half the cooked macaroni in an even layer over the bottom of a casserole dish. Pour the meat mixture evenly over it, then cover with an even layer of the remaining macaroni.

Beat the eggs if using and pour over the top of the macaroni, allowing it to seep through the entire mixture.

Bake in a preheated moderately hot oven, 400°F (200°C/Gas 6), for 40 minutes. Remove from oven and while still hot, sprinkle with grated cheese. Serve warm.

Stuffed tripe Ghammee

As this recipe takes several hours to make, it is generally prepared the day before it is cooked.

Serves 7
Cooking time 4 hours

3 lb (1.5 kg) tripe
1 tablespoon salt
6 pints (4 L) cold water
1 cinnamon stick

STUFFING
$1^1/2$ lb (750 g) ground meat with fat
1 lb (500 g) small whole onions, or quartered large onions
2 teaspoons salt
1 teaspoon mixed spices (see page 15)
1 teaspoon black pepper
$1/4$ teaspoon powdered saffron
$1^1/2$ cups rice, washed and drained
$1/2$ cup chick peas, soaked overnight (see page 14) and cracked with rolling pin
$1/4$ cup water

Mix all stuffing ingredients together and set aside.

Wash the tripe and cut into seven pieces. Place the pieces in boiling water for 1 minute. Wash again in cold water, then rub inside and outside with $1/2$ tablespoon salt.

Using coarse cotton thread, sew the sides of each piece of tripe into a little sack. Fill each sack with stuffing and sew up the opening.

Place the stuffed tripe sacks in a large pot with the water, remaining salt and cinnamon stick. Bring to a boil, skim the surface, reduce heat and simmer until tender, about 4 hours.

When cooked, remove cotton thread and cinnamon stick. Chop up tripe and mix it with stuffing before serving. Alternatively, cut each sack into three slices.

Serve the tripe with the broth, but in separate bowls.

stews

Stews have been popular in the Middle East, as in most other parts of the world, since the earliest times. In Baghdad recipes dating as far back as AD 1226 have been found. In the past stews were always simmered very slowly in a heavy pot on top of a stove or open fire. Today they can be cooked successfully in a covered pot in the oven or in an electric slow-cooker, however pressure cooking does not give good results.

The best meat to use for these stews is mutton, but any type of stewing meat may be substituted. They are generally accompanied by Rice Pilaf or Bur'ghul Pilaf (see page 23).

Dried bean stew Yakh'nit fassoulia

Serves 4
Cooking time 3½ hours

2 cups dried white beans, soaked overnight (see page 14)
2 large onions, finely chopped
2–3 cloves garlic, crushed
1 lb (500 g) stewing meat, cubed
¼ cup ghee or substitute (see page 19)
2 large tomatoes, peeled and chopped
4 tablespoons tomato paste
2½ teaspoons salt
½ teaspoon black pepper
½ teaspoon mixed spices (see page 15)
water

Drain the beans and place in a large saucepan. Cover well with water and bring to a boil, turn down heat and simmer until tender. Drain and set aside.

Lightly brown the onions, garlic and meat in the ghee. Add tomatoes, tomato paste, salt, pepper and spices. Sauté gently for a few minutes. Stir in the cooked beans.

Pour over enough water to just cover. Bring to a boil, turn down the heat, cover and simmer until the meat is very tender or cook as a casserole in a preheated moderate oven for 2–2½ hours. Adjust salt and pepper to taste.

Serve with Rice Pilaf or Bur'ghul Pilaf (see page 23).

Spinach stew Yakh'nit spanigh

Serves 4–6
Cooking time 1¼ hours

1 cup chick peas, soaked overnight (see page 14)
1 lb (500 g) Basic Kafta Mixture (see page 67)
2 tablespoons ghee or substitute (see page 19)
1 lb (500 g) spinach
1 teaspoon salt
½ teaspoon black pepper
2 cloves garlic
1 teaspoon ground coriander

Boil the chick peas, then cover and simmer until tender. Drain and set aside.

Make small balls with the kafta mixture. Brown them lightly in the ghee, using the saucepan in which the stew is to be cooked. Remove from saucepan and set aside.

Place the spinach in the saucepan, cover and simmer gently in its own juice until tender. Add meat balls, chick peas, ½ teaspoon salt and the pepper. Cover and continue to simmer (adding a little water when necessary) until the meat balls are well cooked, about ½ hour.

At the completion of cooking, crush the remainder of the salt with the garlic, add the coriander and fry in a little ghee until the garlic smells sweet. Stir this mixture into the cooked stew. Adjust salt to taste.

Serve with Rice Pilaf (see page 23).

Green bean stew Yakh'nit loobyeh

Serves 6
Cooking time 2½ hours

1 lb (500 g) fresh green string beans
1 lb (500 g) stewing meat, cubed
several meat bones
1½ cups chopped onions
½ cup ghee or substitute (see page 19)
1½ teaspoons salt
½ teaspoon pepper
½ teaspoon mixed spices (see page 15)
2 tablespoons tomato paste blended with 2½ cups water or
   1 x 14 oz (445 g) can tomato soup blended with 2 cups water
2 cloves garlic
1 teaspoon ground coriander

String the beans. Slice down the centre or leave whole.

Lightly brown the meat, bones and onions in the ghee, using the pot in which the stew is to be cooked. Mix in the beans and fry for a few minutes. Add the salt, pepper and mixed spices, then pour in the tomato paste or soup diluted with water. Bring to a boil, then cover and simmer slowly until the meat is very tender.

Crush the garlic with a pinch of salt and fry with the coriander in a little ghee until the garlic smells sweet. Stir this mixture into the cooked stew.

Serve with Rice Pilaf or Bur'ghul Pilaf (see page 23).

You may substitute peas for beans to make Green Pea Stew.

Okra stew Yakh'nit bamyi

Serves 6
Cooking time 1¼–1¾ hours

1 lb (500 g) fresh okra or 1 x 28 oz (875 g) can okra
1 lb (500 g) stewing meat, cubed
1 large onion, chopped
½ cup ghee or substitute (see page 19)
2 ripe medium tomatoes, peeled and sliced
1½ teaspoons salt
½ teaspoon black pepper
½ teaspoon mixed spices (see page 15)
3 tablespoons tomato paste blended with 2 cups water
2 cloves garlic
1 teaspoon ground coriander
2 tablespoons lemon juice

Wash the fresh okra, and cut off the stems.

Lightly brown the meat and onion in ghee, using the pot in which the stew is to be cooked. Add the fresh okra and fry gently for a few minutes.

Mix in tomatoes and simmer for a few minutes. Season with salt, pepper and mixed spices. Add the tomato paste diluted with water and bring to a boil. Cover and simmer until meat is tender, adding more water if necessary.

Crush the garlic with a little salt and fry with the coriander in 1 tablespoon of ghee until the garlic smells sweet. Stir this mixture into the cooked stew and add the lemon juice.

Canned okra may be used, but do not add until meat is tender.

Darweesh rosary Mas'bahet ed'darweesh

Serves 4
Cooking time 2 hours

½ cup ghee or substitute (see page 19)
2 medium onions, chopped
2 cloves garlic, crushed
1 lb (500 g) stewing meat, cubed
1 large eggplant, peeled, cubed and prepared for cooking
   (see page 14)
1 large potato, sliced
5 medium tomatoes, peeled and chopped
1 teaspoon salt
¼ teaspoon pepper
½ teaspoon mixed spices (see page 15)

In the hot ghee, brown the onions, garlic, meat, eggplant, potato and tomatoes. Add salt, pepper, spices and enough water to cover. Pour into a baking pan and bake in a preheated moderate oven, 350°F (180°C/Gas 4), stirring at intervals, until meat and vegetables are tender, about 1¾ hours.

When the vegetables and meat are cooked, transfer to top of stove and simmer uncovered until excess sauce evaporates. Adjust salt and pepper to taste. Serve hot.

Meat and yoghurt stew Lubban oummu

Serves 8
Cooking time 1½ hours

2 lb (1 kg) stewing meat (preferably lamb), cut into large
   pieces
8 small whole white onions, peeled, or 2 medium onions,
   quartered
2 teaspoons salt
½ teaspoon pepper
1 cinnamon stick
2½ cups Cooked Yoghurt, omitting garlic (see page 21)
2 cloves garlic
1 tablespoon ghee or substitute (see page 19)
1 teaspoon ground coriander

Place the meat and onions in a saucepan, add salt,
pepper and cinnamon stick. Cover with water and bring
to a boil.Cover and simmer until the meat is very
tender and most of the water has been evaporated. If
too much water is left after the meat is cooked, drain
some of it. Remove cinnamon stick.

Bring yoghurt to a boil and add to the meat and
onions while they are still simmering. Continue to
simmer uncovered for 15 minutes. Crush garlic with a
little salt and fry it in ghee with the coriander until the
garlic smells sweet. Stir into stew. Adjust seasoning.

Serve hot with Rice Pilaf or Bur'ghul Pilaf (see
page 23).

lenten dishes

Until modern times only stored grain and dried vegetables were available for food in the mountain areas of Lebanon during the cold winters. This factor, together with the country's religious background which forbids the eating of meat, eggs or milk foods during Lent and other religious periods, resulted in the origination of many meat and dairy-free recipes. Some Lenten recipes are hundreds of years old. Fool m'Dammas, for example (right), dates back to at least the Middle Ages. It was originally known as "poor man's food", but is today one of the most popular dishes in Lebanon.

This chapter contains recipes for the basic Lenten dishes. Further Lenten recipes are included in other chapters and can be readily identified by the symbol **L**.

Dried beans in lemon juice Fool m'dammas

Serves 4   **V**   **L**
Cooking time 45 minutes

1 lb (500 g) small dried broad/fava beans, soaked overnight (see page 14)
2 cloves garlic, crushed
1/2 cup olive oil
juice of 1 lemon
1 teaspoon salt
1/4 teaspoon black pepper

Drain the beans and place in a large saucepan. Cover well with water and bring to a boil. Cover, turn down heat and simmer, adding more water and stirring when necessary, until the beans are tender, about 3/4 hour. Drain the beans and mix in the crushed garlic, olive oil, lemon juice, salt and pepper. Serve hot or cold.

Green beans in oil Loob'yeh b'zait

Serves 4–6   V   L
Cooking time 50 minutes

1 lb (500 g) fresh green string beans
$^3/_4$ cup olive oil
2 medium brown onions, finely chopped
1 teaspoon salt
$^1/_2$ teaspoon black pepper
1–2 cups water

String and slice the beans lengthwise.
Heat the olive oil in a saucepan and fry the onions until they are reddish-brown. Mix in the beans, salt and pepper. Sauté for 10 minutes.

Stir in the water, cover and simmer very gently, adding more water if necessary, until the beans are very soft. Remove lid and continue to simmer, uncovered, to absorb excess juice, about 10 minutes.

When cooked the beans should be very brown and soft. Adjust salt and pepper to taste.

To eat these beans the Lebanese way, hold a fork in one hand and push portions onto small pieces of Lebanese bread held in the other hand.

Dried beans with onions Fassoolia humra

Borlotti and salluggia beans can be purchased from most health food stores and many delicatessens and supermarkets.

Serves 4–6   V   L
Cooking time 2½ hours

2 cups borlotti or salluggia beans, soaked overnight (see page 14)
2 large onions, finely chopped
$^1/_2$ cup olive oil
2 teaspoons salt
$^1/_2$ teaspoon black pepper
1 teaspoon mixed spices (see page 15)
4 cups water
1 teaspoon dried mint

Drain beans. In a large saucepan, fry the onions in half the oil until very dark brown. Add the remainder of oil, the beans, salt, pepper and mixed spices. Sauté for a few minutes. Mix in the water, bring to a boil and boil vigorously for 10 minutes. Turn down the heat, cover tightly and simmer, stirring regularly and adding more water if necessary, until the beans are tender and the fliquid is reduced, about 1½ –2½ hours.

If the fluid is not reduced when the beans have become tender, boil vigorously uncovered until it does reduce. Mix in the dried mint.

Serve hot or cold.

Okra in oil Bameh b'zait

Serves 4   V   L
Cooking time about 1½ hours for fresh okra,
   ½ hour for canned okra

2 lb (1 kg) fresh young okra or 1 x 28 oz (875 g) can okra
   with liquid
¼ cup olive oil
12 very small white onions, peeled and left whole
2–3 cloves garlic, halved
1 lb (500 g) tomatoes, skinned and sliced
2 teaspoons salt
¼ teaspoon black pepper
½ cup water
1 lemon

Remove stems from the fresh okra then wash and dry
the okra. Fry okra in the oil in a saucepan until lightly
brown. Remove and set aside on paper towels.

Fry the onions and garlic in the same oil until
slightly brown. Return the okra to the saucepan and
add the tomatoes, salt, pepper and water. Stirring
gently, bring to a boil. Cover tightly, turn down the heat
and simmer very gently until okra are tender, about
¾–1 hour for fresh okra but much less for the canned
variety.

When okra are tender, squeeze in the lemon juice
and continue to simmer for a further 5 minutes. Adjust
salt and pepper to taste.

Serve hot, or let cool in the saucepan and serve
cold, with bread or Rice Pilaf (see page 23).

Endive leaves in oil Hindbeh b'zait

Serves 6   V   L
Cooking time ½–1 hour

1 large bunch endive (about the size of a large lettuce)
2 large onions, chopped
¾ cup olive oil
salt

Wash and chop the endive leaves, then boil in a large
pot of boiling water until tender, about ½–1 hour. Drain
and squeeze out excess water from the leaves with the
palms of the hands, forming large balls. Undo the balls,
and spread on a platter.

Fry the onions in the oil until golden. Remove half
the onions and set aside.

Add the endive leaves and salt to the onions and oil
in the pan and sauté for 10 minutes, stirring constantly.
Turn out onto a platter and cover with the remaining
onions.

Serve hot or cold with bread or in a sandwich.

Spicy dried bean patties Falafel

Makes 35 patties   V   L
Cooking time 5 minutes per batch

$^3/_4$ lb (375 g) broad/fava beans, soaked overnight (see
    page 14)
$^3/_4$ lb (375 g) chick peas, soaked overnight (see page 14)
2 cloves garlic, crushed
1 large brown onion, finely chopped
4 large spring onions, finely chopped
$^1/_2$ hot red or green pepper, finely chopped or ground
1 level tablespoon bicarbonate of soda
3 tablespoons plain flour
1 cup finely chopped parsley
1 teaspoon ground coriander
$^1/_2$ teaspoon ground cumin
$1^1/_2$ tablespoons salt
$^1/_2$ teaspoon black pepper
oil, for frying

Drain the beans and chick peas and rinse well in cold
water. If the beans are not skinless, skin them. Pound
or grind the beans and chick peas (if grinding, put them
through the fine blade of the mincer twice). Mix in the
crushed garlic, chopped onion, spring onions and hot
pepper, then add the remaining ingredients except oil.
Pound or blend the mixture to a smooth paste and let
rest for at least 1 hour.

Take walnut-sized lumps of the mixture and mould
into round flat shapes $1^1/_2$ in (4 cm) in diameter. Allow
to rest for 15 minutes, then deep-fry patties in oil until
golden brown.

Serve hot, accompanied by a tomato and cucumber
salad and Tahini Sauce (see page 18).

Variation Roll the patties in sesame seeds before
frying.

Lentil and rice pilaf M'judra byda

Serves 6–8   V   L
Cooking time 1 hour

$1^1/_4$ cups lentils (see page 15)
2 large onions
1 cup olive or nut oil
6 cups water
2 cups rice, washed and drained
1 tablespoon salt

Prepare and wash lentils as directed on page 15. Slice
onions finely into half circles, place in frying pan with
hot oil and fry until golden brown. Remove half the
onions from the pan and place on paper towels to
drain and become crisp. Leave the remaining onions in
the pan.

Boil lentils in the water until nearly tender, about
20–25 minutes. Mix in rice and bring back to a boil.

Reheat the remaining onions and oil in the frying
pan until very hot. Pour them, with the oil, onto the
boiling lentils and rice. Add salt, cover tightly, turn
down the heat and simmer gently until the rice is
tender and all the liquid is absorbed, about 20 minutes.

Serve hot or cold, garnished with the crisp brown
onion slices. If served cold, accompany with a tossed
salad.

stuffed vegetables

Stuffed vegetables are very popular throughout the Middle East and each country has developed its own variations. They are known as dolma in Turkey, dolmathes in Greece, dolmeh in Persia and mihshi in the Arab lands.

In Lebanon mihshi dishes are made with both meat and Lenten fillings. We have given the traditional recipes for each vegetable. However, they often vary slightly from season to season and from town to town. The ideal size for zucchini and eggplant for stuffing is approximately 4–6 in (10–15 cm) long 1½–2 in (4–5 cm) in diameter. Mihshi are generally served with a variety of other dishes as part of the main course, but they may also be served as a meal in themselves. The usual accompaniments are bread and salad, and sometimes kibbi or yoghurt.

To cook stuffed vegetables

When the stuffed vegetables have been packed tightly in the saucepan as directed in the individual recipes, take a heatproof plate and turn it upside-down over the top of the vegetables, pressing down firmly. Add enough water to cover the plate while it is under pressure.

Leave the plate in place and cover the saucepan securely. Bring quickly to a boil, turn down heat and simmer gently until the vegetables and stuffings are tender and the liquid has reduced and thickened. For maximum flavour leave vegetables to cool in saucepan with juices. Reheat before serving. To serve, drain the juice from the saucepan. Turn the stuffed vegetables onto a large platter and pour the juice over the top.

Stuffed tomatoes Mihshi banadoura

Serves 3–6
Cooking time 1 hour

6 large firm tomatoes
2 cups Meat and Nut Filling (see page 22)
1 tablespoon tomato paste
1 teaspoon salt
black pepper
2 tablespoons ghee or substitute (see page 19)

Wash the tomatoes and cut a thin slice off the top of each one. Scoop out the pulp and set aside.

Fill the tomatoes with the filling, replace the tops and arrange close together on a baking dish.

Sieve the tomato pulp and mix in the tomato paste, salt and pepper. Pour over the tomatoes. Dob each tomato with ghee or substitute and bake in a pre-heated moderate oven until tomatoes are very soft, about 30 minutes.

Serve with Rice Pilaf and Bur'ghul Pilaf (see page 23) as a main dish, or alternatively serve as an accompanying vegetable.

Stuffed spinach leaves Warra mihshi sil'ih

This recipe requires only the spinach leaves. Use the stalks for the salad recipe on page 99.

Serves 6   V   L
Cooking time 1 hour

3 lb (1.5 kg) fresh spinach
4 cups Lenten Stuffing (see page 22)
2 tomatoes, sliced
2 cloves garlic
¼ cup lemon juice
1½ teaspoons salt

Remove the stalks from the spinach. Soften the spinach leaves by dipping in boiling water. Cut into sections about 4 in (10 cm) square.

Place 2 teaspoons of stuffing on each spinach square. Roll up from the bottom and turn in the sides to form a roll about 2½ in (6 cm) long.

Place the tomato slices and garlic cloves in a layer on the bottom of the saucepan. Add the spinach rolls in tightly packed rows and layers, with open ends down. Sprinkle each layer with lemon juice and salt.

Cook as directed on page 84.

Variation Grape vine leaves can be used instead of spinach.

Stuffed grape vine leaves Mihshi warra enib

Serves 6
Cooking time 1½ hours

1 medium brown onion, chopped (optional)
several lean meat bones, for bottom of saucepan (optional)
1 tablespoon ghee or substitute (see page 19)
3 cloves garlic
1 lb (500 g) fresh, tender grape vine leaves
4 cups Meat and Rice Stuffing (see page 22)
½ teaspoon salt
½ cup lemon juice
1 teaspoon dried mint

Lightly brown the onion and meat bones in the ghee using the saucepan in which the vine leaves are to be cooked. Drain off the ghee but leave the onion and bones in the bottom of the saucepan and add 2 cloves of garlic. Cover with a layer of vine leaves.

Soften the remaining vine leaves by dipping a few at a time in boiling water. Taking one leaf at a time, lay it don a work surface with the rough side up and place 1 teaspoon of stuffing in the centre. Fold the bottom of the leaf over the stuffing, then fold it in from each side to the centre. Roll tightly, forming a roll about 3–4 in (7.5–10 cm) long and ½–1 in (1.25–2.5 cm) thick.

Pack the rolls, open ends down, in tight rows and layers in the saucepan, on top of the layer of leaves covering the bones and onions. Sprinkle each layer with salt and lemon juice. Crush the remaining garlic clove, mix it with the remainder of the lemon juice and pour over the last layer of rolls. Sprinkle with mint.

Cook as directed on page 84.

Variation Add 1 finely chopped tomato to the stuffing and include 2 medium-sized sliced tomatoes in the bottom of the saucepan before cooking.

Stuffed zucchini in tomato sauce
Mihshi kousa b'banadoura

The zucchini pulp is not required for this recipe. Use it for Zucchini and Egg Fritters (see page 95) or to enrich soups and stews.

Serves 6
Cooking time 1½ hours

18 small or 12 medium zucchini
4 cups Meat and Rice Stuffing (see page 22)
2 medium onions, finely chopped
4–5 tablespoons ghee or substitute (see page 19)
2–4 cloves garlic
2 tomatoes, sliced
1½ teaspoons salt
2 tablespoons tomato paste or 14½ oz (455 g) can
   tomatoes
4 cups water
1 teaspoon dried mint

Wash the zucchini and cut off the tops, just below the stems. Scoop out the pulp (see page 17) being careful not to break the skin: the other end must remain closed.

Rinse and drain the hollow zucchini. Fill each one three-fourths full with stuffing, allowing for rice expansion.

Lightly brown the onions in the ghee using the saucepan in which the zucchini are to be cooked. Add the garlic and sliced tomatoes to the onions and ghee, covering the bottom of the saucepan evenly. Place the zucchini over the tomatoes, in closely packed rows and layers, sprinkling salt between each layer.

Mix the tomato paste or soup with the water and pour over the zucchini. Sprinkle with mint.

Turn a heatproof dinner plate upside-down over the zucchini to keep them in place and keep in the steam. Cover the saucepan. Bring to a boil, turn down the heat and simmer very gently until the zucchini shells are tender and the filling cooked, about 1–1½ hours.

When cooked, keep the zucchini covered and allow to cool in the juice. Reheat before serving.

To serve, drain the juice from the saucepan into another container. Gently place the zucchini on a platter and pour the juice over the top. Serve as a complete meal with side salad and bread.

Variations For a richer flavour, some bones and a few pieces of stewing meat may be browned with the onions and left in the bottom of the saucepan to cook with the zucchini.

The zucchini may be replaced by eggplant of the same size: this dish is called Batinjaan Mihshi or the zucchini may be replaced by chokoes.

Cabbage rolls Mihshi malfouf

Serves 6
Cooking time 1½ hours

1 medium cabbage
1 large onion, chopped (optional)
several lean meat bones for bottom of saucepan (optional)
1 tablespoon ghee or substitute (see page 19)
5 cloves garlic
4 cups Meat and Rice Stuffing (see page 22)
1½ tablespoons salt
½ cup lemon juice
1 teaspoon dried mint

Remove the core from the cabbage, then separate and wash leaves. Dip them into boiling water a few at a time until they become wilted and pliable. Trim the large central veins flat (removing them if they are too hard to roll). Cut very large leaves in half but leave small ones whole.

Lightly brown the onion and bones in ghee using the saucepan in which the cabbage rolls are to be cooked. Drain off the ghee but leave the onion and bones in the bottom of the saucepan and add 3 cloves of garlic. Cover with one layer of cabbage leaves.

Take one of the remaining cabbage leaves at a time, lay it on a work surface with the inside up and place 1 tablespoon of stuffing in the centre. Fold the bottom of the leaf over the stuffing, then roll tightly, forming a roll about 4–6 in (10–15 cm) long and 1–1½ in (2.5–4 cm) wide. (Please note that in the image on page 88 the ends have been trimmed to illustrate stuffing.)

Pack the rolls, open ends down, in tight rows and layers in the saucepan, on top of the cabbage leaves covering the onions and bones. Sprinkle each layer with salt and lemon juice. Crush the remainder of the garlic, mix with the remainder of the lemon juice and pour over the last layer of rolls. Sprinkle with mint.

Cook as directed on page 84.

Variation Dispense with the onion and meat bones and pack rolls directly over a layer of thick cabbage leaves.

Stuffed zucchini in yoghurt sauce Mihshi kousa b'lubban

Serves 4–6
Cooking time 1½ hours

18 small or 12 medium zucchini
4 cups Meat and Rice Stuffing (see page 22)
1½ teaspoons salt or to taste
1 cup water
2 pints (1 L) Cooked Yoghurt (see page 21)
1–2 teaspoons dried mint

Prepare, scoop and stuff the zucchini as in Stuffed Zucchini in Tomato Sauce recipe (see page 87).

Place the zucchini in tight rows and layers in a saucepan, sprinkling salt over each layer. Add the water and bring to a boil. Cover, turn down the heat to very low and simmer gently until the zucchini are tender and the filling cooked, adding a little more water if required.

When the zucchini are cooked, bring the yoghurt to a boil and pour over the zucchini. Keeping the saucepan uncovered, bring the mixture back to a boil and simmer vigorously for 15 minutes, shaking the saucepan from time to time to allow the sauce to penetrate.

When cooked, sprinkle with mint and turn off heat. Cover and allow to stand for at least 30 minutes before serving.

Serve as in recipe for Stuffed Zucchini in Tomato Sauce (see page 87).

Stuffed, fried and baked eggplant
Sheikh el mihshi

Serves 4–6
Cooking time 1 hour 20 minutes

14 small or 8 medium eggplants
$^3/_4$ cup ghee or substitute (see page 19)
4 cups Meat and Nut Filling (see page 22)
$1^1/_2$ cups tomato juice or 1 tablespoon tomato paste blended
  with $1^1/_2$ cups water

Clean eggplant and trim stems to about $^1/_2$ in (1.25 cm). Do not remove hulls. Partially peel, leaving lengthwise strips of alternating peel and flesh.

Fry eggplant in ghee until soft then drain.

Slit each eggplant lengthwise to form a pocket. Gently press several spoonfuls of filling into the slits. Place eggplants in a casserole dish. Pour the tomato juice over the top and sprinkle with salt and pepper.

Cover and simmer the stovetop for 15 minutes and then bake uncovered for 15 minutes in a preheated hot oven to brown the top.

Serve hot in the casserole dish, accompanied by Rice Pilaf or Bur'ghul Pilaf (see page 23).

Stuffed eggplant Mihshi batinjaan orteh

Serves 4–6   V   L
Cooking time $1^1/_4$ hours

12 very small eggplants
4 cups Lenten Stuffing (see page 22)
$^1/_2$ cup water
$^1/_4$ cup olive or nut oil
4 large tomatoes, finely sliced
2 cloves garlic
salt

Scoop out the eggplants as with Stuffed Zucchini in Tomato Sauce (see page 87) and soak the shell in salted water (see page 14).

Moisten the stuffing with $^1/_2$ cup water. Fill the eggplants three-fourths full, allowing for rice expansion.

Heat the oil in a large saucepan. Place half the sliced tomatoes together with the garlic in layers in the bottom of the saucepan. Closely pack the eggplants in layers over the tomatoes. Sprinkle each layer lightly with salt. Place the remainder of the sliced tomatoes over the top of the eggplants.

Cook as directed on page 84.

Variation Eggplants may also be stuffed as for Stuffed Zucchini in Tomato Sauce (see page 87) and Stuffed Zucchini in Yoghurt Sauce (see page 89).

eggs

Eggs are plentiful in Lebanon and much use is made of them. They are prepared in a variety of ways—hard-boiled, fried, as omelettes, or in other dishes—and the flavour is generally enhanced by herbs, spices and flavourings.

Hard-boiled eggs have been relished from early times. They are often served with salad vegetables in an oil and lemon dressing, or on a platter with other foods for a light meal. A favourite recipe is Luffet Byde, in which the eggs are wrapped in a meat kafta mixture and simmered (see page 95).

Omelettes of all types are extremely popular. They are usually cooked in olive oil rather than butter as in other cuisines. Often the mixture is spooned into the pan to make little omelettes or fried in a special pan which has round depressions in its surface for this purpose.

Egg dishes are eaten mainly for breakfast or lunch and are generally accompanied by Lebanese bread and salads.

Fried eggs in olive oil Byde mi'li

Serves 1   **V**
Cooking time 5 minutes

2 eggs
olive oil
¹/₂ lemon
finely chopped fresh or dried mint or oregano

Fry the eggs in very hot olive oil, basting the yolks to give a white film.

Squeeze lemon juice over the top, garnish with mint or oregano and serve immediately, accompanied by Lebanese bread and whole spring onions.

To eat these eggs the Lebanese way, hold a fork in one hand and push bite-sized portions onto small pieces of Lebanese bread held in the other hand.

Eggplant omelette Ijit batinjaan

Serves 4–6   **V**
Cooking time 15–20 minutes

2 small or 1 large eggplant
1 onion, finely chopped
2 tablespoons olive oil or substitute
1–2 cloves garlic, crushed
6 eggs
salt and black pepper

Peel and cube the eggplant, and prepare for cooking as directed on page 14.

Fry the chopped onion in the oil until soft and golden. Add the crushed garlic, then the eggplant and sauté until tender.

Beat the eggs, season with salt and pepper, and stir into the eggplant mixture. Cook over very low heat until the eggs are set.

Brown the top of the omelette under the griller or slip it onto a plate and return to the pan to cook the other side.

Eggs with tomato Byde b'banadoura

Serves 4–6   **V**
Cooking time 20 minutes

4 ripe medium tomatoes
2 tablespoons water
4 eggs
salt and pepper
$1/2$ teaspoon ground cinnamon
$1/2$ cup finely chopped parsley (optional)
$1/4$ cup finely chopped spring onions (optional)
1 tablespoon olive oil or substitute

Wash, peel and quarter the tomatoes. Simmer them gently in the water in a covered pan until soft. Pour into a baking dish.

Beat eggs well and mix in salt, pepper and cinnamon, and parsley and spring onions if using. Pour this mixture over the tomatoes.

Cook over a low heat, without stirring, until the eggs are set. Pour oil over the eggs and place under the griller to brown the top.

Parsley omelettes Ijit b'dounis

Makes 20 small omelettes   **V**
Cooking time about 2 minutes per batch

4 eggs
1 cup chopped parsley or $1/2$ cup mint and $1/2$ cup parsley
1 teaspoon flour
salt and pepper
olive oil or substitute

Beat eggs and combine with dry parsley or mint, flour, salt and pepper. Spoon into hot oil to make small omelettes and cook. Repeat this procedure until all the mixture is used.

Brain omelette Ijit n'kha

Serves 2
Cooking time 35 minutes

2 sets lamb's brains, steamed and sliced
salt and black pepper
3 eggs
2 spring onions, finely chopped
1 tablespoon olive oil or substitute

Sprinkle the sliced brains with salt and pepper. Beat the eggs and season with salt and pepper. Mix in the spring onions.

Gently heat the oil in a frying pan and pour in the egg and onion mixture. Spread the sliced brains evenly over the top and cook over a very low heat until the eggs are just set, about 20 minutes.

Place under a griller or slip the omelette onto a plate and return to the pan to cook the other side.

Egg roll Luffet byde

Serves 4–6
Cooking time 30 minutes

2 cups Basic Kafta Mixture, omitting parsley (see page 67)
1/2 cup finely chopped parsley
3 hard-boiled eggs
1/2 cup ghee or substitute (see page 19)

With wet hands, roll the kafta mixture into a ball and flatten it onto a wet board, forming a flat oblong shape, about 1/2 in (1.25 cm) thick. Sprinkle the parsley over the top.

Shell the eggs and place end to end along the centre of mixture. Roll the mixture around the eggs to form a meat roll, join the ends together and smooth the meat all over with wet hands. Wind a long length of coarse white cotton thread around the roll in all directions to keep the meat together.

Heat the ghee in a saucepan, add the meat roll and cook until well browned all over. Cover, turn down the heat and simmer gently until cooked through, turning the roll regularly and sprinkling a few drops of water over it occasionally to prevent it from drying out, about 20–30 minutes.

When cooked, remove the roll from the saucepan, let cool, then remove the thread. Refrigerate before cutting in slices.

Serve with salads.

Zucchini and egg fritters ljit kousa

Makes about 12   **V**
Cooking time 8–10 minutes per batch

1 clove garlic
1 teaspoon salt
4–6 spring onions
1 pinch pepper
1/4 teaspoon mixed spices (see page 15)
1 cup zucchini pulp
5 eggs
3/4 cup self-raising flour
1/2–1 cup chopped parsley
1/4 cup chopped fresh mint or 1 teaspoon dried mint
olive or nut oil

Crush the garlic in a bowl with the salt. Mix in the spring onions, pepper and mixed spices. Add the mashed zucchini and the eggs. Beat well with a beater, then thoroughly mix in the flour. Add parsley and mint. Spoon the mixture into a pan of hot oil and fry until the fritters are golden brown on both sides. Repeat this procedure until all the mixture is used.

Variation Add 1 tablespoon of olive oil or nut oil to the mixture. Pour it into a greased baking dish to a thickness of 1–1 1/2 in (2.5–4 cm) and bake in a preheated moderate oven until cooked, about 45 minutes.

salads

Salads are an important part of the Lebanese menu. No meal is complete without a platter of crisp salad vegetables or a tossed salad. The king of Lebanese salads is the famous Tabbouleh (right), made with parsley and bur'ghul. Another very popular salad is Fattoush (see page 98), which includes chickweed and toasted cubes of bread and probably originated among the poorer people.

Cooked salads and salads in which some of the ingredients are cooked and others raw are also well liked.

The ingredients for Lebanese salads must be as fresh as possible. They should be washed well and dried, and served cold and crisp. The traditional dressing is a simple combination of lemon juice and olive oil, with garlic, salt and black pepper.

Parsley salad Tabbouleh

Serves 4   **V**   **L**

$1/2$ **cup bur'ghul (see page 14)**
8–10 spring onions
2 teaspoons salt
$1/4$ **teaspoon black pepper**
$1/4$ **teaspoon mixed spices (see page 15)**
5 cups very finely chopped parsley
$1/4$ **cup very finely chopped fresh mint or 2 teaspoons dried mint**
3 large tomatoes, finely chopped
about $1/4$ **cup lemon juice**
$1/4$ **cup olive oil**

Wash the bur'ghul and drain well by squeezing out excess water with cupped hands. Place in a bowl and refrigerate for at least 1 hour.

Trim the spring onions, leaving about 8 in (20 cm) of the green top. Finely chop the white part of the spring onions and mix it into the drained bur'ghul with the salt, pepper and spices. Finely chop the green part of the spring onions and place it with parsley, mint and tomatoes on top of the bur'ghul mixture. Set aside in the refrigerator until ready to serve.

Just before serving, add the lemon juice and olive oil and toss well. Adjust salt and lemon juice to taste.

Tabbouleh is usually served in a wide-based bowl or deep serving dish and garnished with lettuce leaves. When it is served as mezza, a large spoonful is placed in a lettuce leaf, wrapped into a roll and eaten with the fingers.

Variation Add 1 small cucumber or $1/2$ green pepper (both finely chopped) to the salad.

Salad dressing

Makes 1 cup   V   L

¹/₂ cup lemon juice
¹/₂ cup olive oil
2 cloves garlic
1 teaspoon salt
¹/₄ teaspoon black pepper

Mix the lemon juice and oil together. Crush the garlic to a paste with the salt and mix it into the oil and lemon juice. Add pepper.

Peasant salad Fattoush

It is customary, although not essential, to include chickweed (baquli) in this salad. This weed is not sold commercially but grows wild in many gardens. It has soft green leaves and is considered very nourishing.

Serves 6   V   L

1 cup very crisp toasted bread (preferably Lebanese), cubed and sprinkled with a little water
4 small cucumbers or 2 cups shredded lettuce, or half of each
2 medium tomatoes
¹/₂–1 green pepper, finely chopped
¹/₂ cup finely chopped spring onions
¹/₂ cup finely chopped parsley
¹/₄ cup finely chopped mint
1 cup finely chopped chickweed (optional)
¹/₂ cup Salad Dressing (see left)

Place all the ingredients in a bowl and toss well. Add the dressing and toss again. Adjust salt and lemon juice to taste.

Cabbage salad Salatit malfouf

Serves 6–8   V   L

1 small or ¹/₂ large green or red cabbage
¹/₂ teaspoon salt
¹/₂ cup Salad Dressing, omitting salt (see left)

Core the cabbage and remove any tough outer leaves. Shred the cabbage leaves finely and sprinkle with salt. Rub the salt well into the leaves.

Place the salted leaves in a colander, cover with a weighted plate to extract excess moisture and let stand for 30 minutes.

When the cabbage leaves are soft, squeeze them tightly to remove excess moisture and place them in a salad bowl. Pour the dressing over the top and toss well. Adjust salt and lemon juice to taste.

Endive salad Hindbeh m'tabbal

Serves 6   V   L
Cooking time 1/2–1 hour

1 large bunch of endive (about the size of a large lettuce)
1 large onion, finely chopped
1 teaspoon salt
1/4 teaspoon pepper
1/4 cup lemon juice
1/4 cup olive oil

Wash and chop the endive leaves, then boil in a large pot of boiling water until tender, about 1/2–1 hour. Lightly drain and place in a bowl. Add the chopped onion, salt, pepper, lemon juice and olive oil. Toss, let cool and refrigerate before serving.

Cooked vegetable salad Salatit khoodra

Serves 4   V   L

4 cups sliced zucchini, string beans, chokoes or cauliflower
    pieces, or a combination of these
3/4 cup Salad Dressing (see opposite)

Partially cook the vegetables in boiling water. Drain and let cool. Add dressing and toss well. Adjust salt and lemon juice to taste.

Spinach Stalks Dlough silih

This recipe requires only the spinach stalks. Use the leaves for Stuffed Spinach Leaves (see page 86), Spinach Soup (see page 36) or Spinach Stew (see page 74).

Makes about 4 cups   V   L
Cooking time 1/2 hour

1 lb (500 g) spinach stalks (without leaves)
boiling water
2 teaspoons salt
pinch of baking powder
1 cup Tahini Sauce (see page 18)

Chop the spinach stalks into 2-in (5-cm) strips. Place in boiling water with salt and baking powder and simmer until soft and tender, about 50 minutes.

Drain stalks and mash or leave sliced. Gently mix in the Tahini Sauce.

Serve cold.

pickles

Before refrigeration and easy transport, the preservation of food was a great problem in the hot countries of the Middle East, particularly in isolated areas. Pickling was originally devised to overcome this problem, however the result was so delicious that pickles are still an important part of the diet.

Almost every Lebanese household has a selection of homemade pickles. They are an important part of the mezza and are often served as accompaniments for the main course.

The pickling solution we have given uses equal quantities of brine and vinegar, however some people prefer to use all brine or all vinegar or other proportions of the two. Always mix the solution in clean, grease-free glass, porcelain or enamel containers.

For successful pickling you must use prime, fresh vegetables which have been thoroughly washed and dried. Cucumbers and eggplants should be tiny—no more than 4 in x 1 in (10 cm x 2.5 cm)—and can be ordered from your local market or greengrocer.

Store the pickles in sterilised glass or porcelain jars with airtight lids. Ensure that the solution completely covers the vegetables and that there are no air bubbles in the jar. They will keep for about two months.

Pickling solution

Makes 5 cups   **V**   **L**
Cooking time 10 minutes

¹/₂ **cup cooking salt**
2 cups water
2¹/₂ cups vinegar

Stir the salt into the water. Bring to a boil and boil for 3 minutes. Add the vinegar.

Pickled eggplant Kabees batinjaan

Cooking time 40 minutes   **V**   **L**

2 lb (1 kg) very small, thin eggplants
4 cloves garlic
1 teaspoon salt
2 hot peppers
5 cups Pickling Solution (see above)
1 tablespoon olive oil

Wash the eggplants and discard stems. Place the eggplants in a pot of boiling water and bring to a boil. Cover, reduce the heat and simmer for 3 minutes. Remove from the water and allow to drain for about 30 minutes.

Crush the garlic and salt to a paste. Chop 1 hot pepper and mix it into the garlic.

Make a deep lengthwise slit in each side of each eggplant. Put a pinch of the garlic and hot pepper mixture into the slits.

Place the eggplants and the remaining hot pepper in a large sterilised glass jar. Cover with the pickling solution and add olive oil. Seal with an airtight lid and set aside for at least 2 weeks before eating.

Variation Add chopped walnuts to garlic and pepper mixture.

Pickled cucumber Kabees kh'yaar

Cooking time 10 minutes   **V**   **L**

2¹/₂ lb (1.25 kg) very small thin cucumbers
1 hot pepper
5 cups Pickling Solution (see page 100)
1 tablespoon olive oil

Wash and dry the cucumbers and place them in a large sterilised jar with the hot pepper. Cover with the pickling solution and add the olive oil. Seal with an airtight lid and set aside for at least 1 week before eating.

Pickled turnips Kabees lifit

Cooking time 10 minutes   **V**   **L**

2 lb (1 kg) turnips
2 large beetroot (for colour)
1 hot pepper
5 cups Pickling Solution (see page 100)

Peel the turnips and beetroot, wash very well and slice into quarters. Place in a sterilised glass jar with the hot pepper. Cover with pickling solution, seal with an airtight lid and set aside for at least 10 days before eating.

Pickled onions Kabees bassal

V   **L**

2¹/₂ lb (1.25 kg) small firm white onions
1 hot pepper
5 cups Pickling Solution (see page 100)

Peel the onions and place in a sterilised glass jar with the hot pepper. Cover with pickling solution. Seal with an airtight lid and set aside for at least 7–10 days before eating.

Pickled green olives Kabees zeitoon akhdar

V   L

4 lb (2 kg) raw green olives
coarse salt
water
few lemon wedges
1 hot green pepper (optional)

Wash the olives well in lukewarm water. Split each olive two or three times with a sharp fine-bladed knife or leave intact. Place in a sterilised glass or earthenware container and cover with salted water, using ½ cup salt to every 5 pints (2.5 L) of water. Place a small plate on top of the olives to prevent them from floating. Cover and leave to soak for 6–8 weeks, changing the salted water every week.

Make a brine by boiling together 1 cup salt to every 4 cups of water. Allow to cool.

Drain the soaked olives and place in a sterilised glass or earthenware container with the lemon wedges and hot green pepper. Cover with the cool brine, replace the plate and seal with an airtight lid. Set aside for about 6–8 weeks until the bitter taste disappears.

Pickled black olives Kabees zeitoon uswid

V   L

4 lb (2 kg) raw black olives
1 cup coarse salt
½ cup olive oil
½ cup brown vinegar (optional)

Wash the olives well in lukewarm water. Place in a sterilised glass or earthenware container and cover with water. Place on top of the olives to prevent them from floating. Cover and leave to soak for 6 days, changing the water every day.

Drain the soaked olives and place in a sterilised glass or earthenware container. Add the salt, olive oil and vinegar if using and mix well. Seal with an airtight lid and set aside for apbout 2–4 weeks until the bitter taste disappears.

Pickled cauliflower Kabees ar'nabit

Cooking time 20 minutes   **V   L**

1 medium cauliflower
1 large beetroot (for colour)
5 cups Pickling Solution (see page 100)

Break or cut the cauliflower into flowerettes and wash. Place in a pot of water, bring to a boil and simmer for 3 minutes. Drain well and place in sterilised pickling jars.

Wash and peel the beetroot, cut into quarters and add to the cauliflower.

Cover with pickling solution, seal with an airtight lid and set aside for at least 3 days before eating.

sweets

Lebanese cakes, pastries, desserts, jams and preserves are very sweet. They are always served to visitors with coffee, and are often eaten as snacks between meals. However they are not necessarily served as desserts at the end of a meal, but may be replaced by a bowl of fresh fruit in season.

The most popular Lebanese sweets are B'learwa (see page 112) and K'naafeh pastries (see page 110) which, like many recipes, are saturated in a fragrant sugar syrup. They are made commercially, but like most foods they are even more delicious when fresh from the home kitchen.

Some Lebanese sweets are traditionally made to celebrate religious or family festivities. Oo'whamat (see page 109), for example, are made for the Gh'taas (baptism of Christ) celebration, Ma'amool b'Jowz (see page 115) are special Easter cakes, and Meghli (see page 106) is a rice pudding served to well-wishers when a baby is born. Although many sweets appear very intricate, most of them are surprisingly easy to make and with a little practice you can become a real expert.

Plain rice pudding Ruz b'haleeb

Serves 6　　　**V**
Cooking time 45 minutes

3$^{1}/_{2}$ cups milk
$^{1}/_{2}$ cup sugar
$^{1}/_{2}$ cup rice, washed and drained
$^{1}/_{2}$ cup water
1 teaspoon rosewater or orange blossom water (see page 16)
$^{1}/_{2}$ cup blanched slivered almonds, for garnish

Bring the milk and sugar to a boil. Add the rice, the water and stir until it comes to a boil again. Turn down the heat to a low simmer and cook gently until the mixture becomes very creamy, about 45 minutes. (Add a little more milk during cooking if necessary.)

Add the rosewater or orange blossom water, stirring until bubbles appear on the surface.

Remove from the heat and let cool slightly, then pour into a bowl and refrigerate.

Serve chilled, garnished with slivered almonds.

Festive rice pudding Meghli

Serves 8   **V**
Cooking time 1¼ hours

1 cup ground rice, washed and drained
5 cups cold water
1 cup sugar
1 teaspoon aniseed or ½ teaspoon powdered
1 teaspoon fennel seeds or ½ teaspoon powdered
1 teaspoon caraway seeds or ½ teaspoon powdered
2 teaspoons ground cinnamon
½ cup blanched slivered almonds, for garnish

Mix the ground rice to a smooth paste with some of the cold water. Add the sugar, aniseed, fennel, caraway and cinnamon.

Bring the remaining water to a boil. Add the ground rice mixture gradually, stirring vigorously with a wooden spoon. Continue stirring until it comes to a boil again, then simmer until cooked, about 1 hour.

The mixture is cooked when it is thick enough to coat the spoon. Let cool slightly, pour into individual bowls and refrigerate.

Serve chilled, garnished with the almonds.

Ground rice pudding M'hal'labeeyeh

Serves 6–8   **V**
Cooking time 20 minutes

2 tablespoons cornflour/cornstarch
¼ cup ground rice, washed and drained
2½ pints (1.25 L) milk
1 cup sugar
1 teaspoon rosewater or orange blossom water (see page 16)
¼ cup blanched slivered almonds or some Crystallised Flowers for garnish (see page 119)

Mix the cornflour/cornstarch and ground rice to a paste with a little of the milk. Mix the remaining milk with the sugar and bring to a boil. Warm the paste with a few tablespoons of the boiling milk.

Lower the heat to a simmer and, using a wooden spoon, gradually stir the warm paste into the milk. (Be careful not to scrape the bottom of the pot with the spoon so that you do not dislodge particles of burned milk which may have occurred during boiling.)

Continue stirring the mixture until it thickens enough to coat the spoon. Stir for a further 1 minute, then remove from the heat and stir in the rosewater or orange blossom water. Let cool slightly, pour into individual dishes and refrigerate.

Serve chilled, garnished with slivered almonds or Crystallised Flowers.

Syrup cheese Helwhaat el jibni

Serves 4–6   V
Cooking time about 30 minutes

1 lb (500 g) unsalted mature white Lebanese cheese or
  unsalted mozzarella cheese
1½ cups boiling water
1½ cups semolina
2 cups hot Sugar Syrup (see right)

Slice the cheese. Place the water in a saucepan and bring it to a boil. Gently stir in the sliced cheese until it melts (only a few seconds), then drain all but 1 or 2 tablespoons of the water.

Return the cheese to the heat and stir with a wooden spoon, gradually adding the semolina. Then gradually stir in ¼ cup of hot syrup over a low heat for about 3 minutes, making sure that you stir it vigorously to avoid sticking.

Lightly moisten a baking tray with about 2 tablespoons of the hot syrup. Remove the hot cheese mixture (it will resemble dough) from the stovetop and quickly pour it onto the moistened tray. Wearing rubber gloves to protect the hands from the heat, quickly flatten the cheese dough into a paper-thin sheet over the bottom of the tray.

Sprinkle a little more syrup over the dough in the baking tray, fold the edges of the sheet into the centre and then again until it becomes a square lump. Flatten out the lump again into a thin sheet, moistening with more syrup if necessary. The dough should now resemble a piece of fine cloth. Tear the "cloth" into strips and drop them into the remainder of the warm syrup. Serve cool or chilled, plain or with Ushta (see page 20).

Sugar syrup Atter

This syrup will keep well if stored in an airtight jar. When used for sweetening pastries, it should be cold and poured over very hot pastry, otherwise it will not penetrate the pastry.

Makes 3 cups   V
Cooking time 10 minutes

3 cups sugar
1½ cups water
1 tablespoon lemon juice
1 teaspoon rosewater or orange blossom water (see
  page 16)

Dissolve sugar in water, add lemon juice and bring to a boil. Skim the foam from the surface and continue to boil, stirring occasionally until syrup thickens slightly, about 10 minutes. Add the rosewater or orange blossom water towards the end of the cooking time.

Let syrup stand to cool.

Dough balls in syrup Oo'whamat

Makes about 50 balls   **V**
Cooking time 5 minutes per batch

3¹/₂ cups plain flour
¹/₄ oz (7.5 g) dried yeast or ¹/₂ oz (15 g) fresh yeast
2¹/₂ cups lukewarm water
1 teaspoon sugar
nut or corn oil, for frying
4 cups Sugar syrup (see page 107)
ground cinnamon (optional)

Warm a mixing bowl and sift the flour into it.

Dissolve the yeast in ¹/₄ cup of the lukewarm water, add the sugar and set aside until it rises and foams.

Beat the remaining water into the yeast, then gradually add the flour, beating constantly until the mixture becomes a sticky batter. Cover with a damp cloth and place in a warm spot to rise, about 1¹/₄ hours. During the first hour beat the mixture vigorously at 15 minute intervals.

Place 2 in (5 cm) oil in a frying pan and heat until very hot. With a wet teaspoon, scoop up the dough and drop it into the hot oil. The dough balls will swell up and float to the top, at which stage you should turn down the heat to medium and keep cooking until they are crisp and golden brown.

Remove the dough balls from the oil, drain on paper towels, and while still hot immerse briefly in cool Sugar syrup. Set aside and sprinkle with cinnamon.

Serve hot or cold.

Date Walnut Delights Kark b'tamar wa jowz

Serves 8   **V**
Cooking time 20–30 minutes

8 oz (250 g) butter
1 cup coarsely chopped dates
1 cup walnuts, broken into large pieces
1 cup raw sugar
2 full cups self-raising flour
¹/₂ teaspoon ground cinnamon
icing sugar

Melt the butter and let cool. In a large bowl, mix together the dates, walnuts, raw sugar, flour and cinnamon. Add the melted butter and knead the mixture into a dough with your hands. Take large walnut-sized balls of the dough and mould them into elongated shapes by squeezing gently in the palm of your hand. Cook on an ungreased baking tray in a preheated moderate oven at 350°F (180°C/Gas 4) until lightly brown, for 20–30 minutes. When cool, remove from the tray and liberally sift icing sugar over the balls.

Sweets

K'naafeh Pastry

Already prepared k'naafeh pastry can be purchased from Lebanese bakeries and delicatessens, and from some continental delicatessens. The recipe is extremely intricate and is not usually made in the home. It is included here for the keen and the curious. The pastry should resemble white vermicelli. To make it you will need a k'naafeh strainer, which is a metal container with a line of holes in the bottom to allow the batter to pour through in fine threads.

2 lb (1 kg) plain flour
2 cups water
1¼ cups milk

Mix ingredients together and knead into a smooth dough. Gradually add enough water to form a thin batter.

Heat a heavy griddle over a low heat and pour the batter onto it, passing it first through a k'naafeh strainer. The batter will come through the strainer in long stringlike strips and solidify on the hot griddle.

As soon as the k'naafeh strips are set, remove and set aside. Continue making more strips until all the batter is used.

String pastry sweets K'naafeh

Serves 8   V
Cooking time 55 minutes

6½ oz (200 g) k'naafeh pastry, bought or homemade (see left)
½ cup ghee (see page 19) or unsalted butter, melted
2 cups cold rosewater or orange blossom water (see page 16)

VANILLA CREAM FILLING
¾ cup cornflour/cornstarch
1½ pints (750 ml) milk
⅓ pint (150 ml) cream
2 teaspoons vanilla essence

Place the k'naafeh pastry in a large bowl and separate the "strings" as much as possible. Pour in the melted ghee or butter and work it in with the fingers, making sure that each pastry string is thoroughly greased. (Traditionally the string is now put through a grinder and crumbled, however it is just as delicious when left whole.)

Vanilla cream filling Make a paste with the cornflour/cornstarch and some of the milk, and set aside. Heat the milk and cream together in a saucepan. Remove from the heat and mix a little of the hot milk and cream into the cornflour paste to warm, then pour the paste into the hot milk mixture, stirring constantly. Return to the heat and simmer until thick, stirring constantly to avoid lumps. (If it does get lumpy, use an eggbeater.) Mix in the vanilla essence.

To assemble the k'naafeh Place half the pastry strings evenly over the bottom of a 10-in (25-cm) baking dish and cover with the filling, then place the remainder of the pastry in an even layer on top and press down firmly.

Bake in a preheated oven at 350°F (180°C/Gas 4) for 45 minutes, then turn up to 450°F (230°C/Gas 8) and bake for a further 10–15 minutes or until light golden on top.

Remove from oven and while still hot, pour cool rosewater or orange blossom water over. Serve hot or cold.

Variation Crumbled unsalted Lebanese white cheese, mozzarella or ricotta can be substituted for the vanilla cream filling.

Lebanese pancakes Atayif

Serves 8   **V**
Cooking time apbout 8 minutes each

BATTER
1¹/₂ oz (45 g) fresh yeast or ¹/₄ oz (7.5 g) dried yeast
1 teaspoon sugar
1¹/₂ cups lukewarm water
1¹/₂ cups plain flour

TOPPING
3 cups cold Sugar Syrup (see page 107)

Dissolve the yeast and sugar together in ¹/₂ cup of the lukewarm water. Let stand in a warm place until it begins to bubble, about 10 minutes.

Sift the flour into a warm bowl and make a well in the centre, then pour in the yeast mixture and rub it into the flour.

Pour the remainder of the lukewarm water into the flour mixture and stir until it is a smooth batter. Cover with a cloth and let stand in a warm place for 1 hour or until the batter rises and is bubbly.

Thoroughly grease the inside of a heavy frying pan by rubbing it with a paper towel dipped in oil, then heat until very hot. Turn down the heat to medium and drop 1 tablespoon of batter into the pan. Gently tilt the pan from side to side to help the batter spread evenly, but make sure it remains round and thick. When the pancake begins to bubble and comes away easily from the pan, flip it over and cook the other side. Repeat this process until all the batter is used.

As the pancakes are cooked, pile them on a plate, one on top of the other. While still hot, dip each one into cold Sugar syrup and serve, either by themselves or accompanied by Ushta (see page 20) or whipped cream sprinkled with chopped nuts.

Stuffed lebanese pancakes Atayif mihshi

Serves 8   **V**
Cooking time about 10 minutes

1 quantity Lebanese Pancake batter (see left)
2 cups finely chopped walnuts mixed with 3 tablespoons
   sugar and 2 teaspoons ground cinnamon
3 cups cold Sugar Syrup (see page 107)
olive or nut oil, for frying

Make pancakes from batter as in previous recipe, but cook one side only. Set aside, one on top of the other, until all are cooked.

Cover the uncooked side of each pancake with the walnut and sugar mixture, then fold into semicircles and pinch the edges to secure.

Deep-fry the stuffed pancakes in hot oil until a golden colour, about 2–3 minutes. Drain well on paper towels and while still hot, dip in the cold Sugar syrup. Serve hot or cold.

Variations Substitute one of the following fillings for the walnut mixture: 2 cups Ushta (see page 20);
1 lb (500 g) unsalted Lebanese white cheese, grated;
1 lb (500 g) Ricotta cheese

String pastry rolls Boorrma

Makes 15 rolls   **V**

6½ oz (200 g) k'naafeh pastry, commercial or homemade
   (see page 110)
¼ lb (125 g) ghee (see page 19) or unsalted butter, melted
1 cup walnut pieces or a mixture of walnuts, almonds and
   pistachio nuts, finely chopped or coarsely ground
1½ tablespoons sugar
1½ cups cold Sugar syrup (see page 107)

Prepare the k'naafeh pastry for cooking by greasing
well with the melted ghee or butter as in the recipe for
String Pastry Sweets (see page 110), but leave the
strings whole.

Mix the chopped nuts with the sugar. Divide the
k'naafeh pastry into strands about 8 in (20 cm) long
and 2½ in (6.5 cm) wide. Place 1 tablespoon of the nut
mixture on the top of 1 strand. Put the round handle of
a wooden spoon over the mixture and roll the pastry
around it to form a roll. Remove the spoon handle.
Continue until all the rolls are made.

Place rolls on a baking tray and bake in a moderate
oven until golden, about 20–25 minutes. Remove from
the oven and pour the Sugar syrup over the rolls.

Sweet layered pastries B'learwa

Makes 28 pieces   **V**
Cooking time 35 minutes

½ lb (250 g) melted butter, preferably unsalted
1 lb (500 g) filo pastry
2 cups walnut pieces or a mixture of walnuts, almonds and
   pistachio nuts, finely chopped or coarsely ground
3 tablespoons sugar
1½ cups cold Sugar Syrup (see page 107)

Using a pastry brush, paint the sides and bottom of a
round or square baking dish, about 12 in x 18 in
(30 cm x 45 cm) in size, with butter.

Paint one of the pastry sheets with butter and place
it in the baking tray, then paint a second sheet and
place it on top of the first, overlapping or folding in the
sides of the sheet if necessary. Continue in this way
until half the amount of sheets have been buttered
(6 or more layers).

Mix the chopped nuts with the sugar and spread
evenly over the top sheet of pastry in the tray. Cover
with the remaining pastry sheets, buttering them as for
the lower layers. Be sure to brush the top of the final
sheet with butter.

Cut deep diagonal lines down and across the
surface of the pastry to form diamond-shaped slices.

Bake on the centre shelf of a preheated oven at
325–350°F (170–180°C/Gas 3–4) for 30 minutes, then
increase the temperature to 450–475°F (230–240°C/
Gas 8–9) and bake for a further 5–10 minutes, or until
the pastry puffs and is a light golden colour. Remove
from the oven and while still hot, pour the cold sugar
syrup over it.

Variation Butter and stack the pastry as above until the
stack is ¼ in (7 mm) thick. Cut the stack into 3-in
(7.5-cm) squares. Draw up the edges of each square
and pinch the corners to form shells. Fill each shell
with nut and sugar mixture.

Semolina and yoghurt slices Mummoora

Makes 15 slices　　**V**
Cooking time about 50 minutes

2¹/₂ cups semolina
2 cups yoghurt
¹/₂ cup sugar
¹/₄ lb (125 g) butter, melted
1 teaspoon baking powder
2 cups cool Sugar Syrup (see page 107)

Mix together the semolina, yoghurt, sugar, butter and baking powder. Spread the mixture evenly in a well-greased baking tray, about 10 in (25 cm) in size, and bake in a 350°F (180°C/Gas 4) oven until cooked through and lightly brown on top, about 50 minutes.

Remove from the oven and while still hot, cut diagonal lines through the cooked mixture to make diamond-shaped pieces, then pour the cool sugar syrup over the top.

Serve hot or cold, either by itself or with Ushta (see page 20) or whipped cream.

Variation Substitute ¹/₂ cup desiccated coconut for ¹/₂ cup of the semolina. Garnish each piece with an almond.

Orange and coconut cake Kark el laemoon jose el hind

Cooking time 45 minutes　　**V**

¹/₂ lb (250 g) butter
¹/₄ cup sugar
4 eggs
¹/₄ teaspoon baking powder
1 cup self-raising flour
1 cup semolina
1¹/₂ cups desiccated coconut
1¹/₂ teaspoons ground cinnamon
1 tablespoon grated orange peel
¹/₂ cup walnut pieces
¹/₂ cup orange juice
¹/₄ cup sweet wine or sherry (optional)
¹/₂ cup blanched slivered almonds
3 cups cold Sugar Syrup (see page 107)

Cream butter and sugar, and gradually beat in the eggs.

Sift the baking powder with the flour and mix in the semolina, 1 cup of the desiccated coconut, the cinnamon, orange peel and walnuts.

With a wooden spoon, lightly stir the dry ingredients into the creamed butter, adding orange juice and wine or sherry if using. Pour into a well-greased and lightly floured baking dish, about 9 in (23 cm) in size. Garnish with slivered almonds and bake in a preheated oven at 350°F (180°C/Gas 4) for 45 minutes.

When the cake is cooked and golden brown on top, remove it from the oven and while still hot, spoon the sugar syrup over the top. Sprinkle with the remaining ¹/₂ cup of desiccated coconut.

Easter walnut cakes Ma'amool b'Jowz

Makes 12–13 small cakes   **V**
Cooking time 20 minutes

PASTRY
1¹/₂ lb (750 g) semolina
1 cup sugar
1 lb (500 g) butter
boiling water

FILLING
1 lb (500 g) fresh walnut pieces
¹/₂ cup sugar
¹/₂ teaspoon rosewater (see page 16)
¹/₄ cup cold water

TOPPING
2 cups icing sugar

Pastry Place the semolina and sugar in a large bowl and mix together thoroughly.

Melt the butter and bring it to a boil, then gradually blend it into the semolina and sugar mixture. Knead well, then set aside in an airtight container for at least 1 hour or up to 24 hours.

Knead the mixture again, pouring in enough boiling water to make a soft pliable dough. (It is a good idea to wear rubber gloves to protect your hands from the heat.)

Filling Crush the walnuts into very small pieces and mix in the sugar.

Add the rosewater to the cold water and mix into the walnut and sugar mixture.

To make cakes Mould the pastry into small balls about 2 in (5 cm) in diameter. Hollow out the centre of each ball with your index finger by pressing around the inside of the ball to make a shell about ¹/₄ in (7 mm) thick. Fill the hollow shell with the filling mixture and close the top of the shell by pressing the dough together.

Flatten the shell into a pie shape by pressing lightly between the palms of the hands. Make a design on top with the side and prongs of a fork. (A special mould called a taabeh can be used if you prefer.)

Place the cakes on a baking tray and cook in a preheated very hot oven, 450°F (230°C/Gas 8), until lightly browned, about 20 minutes.

Topping Sprinkle sifted icing sugar generously over the top of the cakes. Store in airtight containers.

Sesame seed biscuits Biscorti el soom soom

Makes about 45 biscuits   **V**
Cooking time 20–25 minutes

1/2 lb (250 g) butter or margarine
3/4 cup sugar
3 teaspoons vanilla essence
1 egg
1/3 cup milk
4 1/2 cups self-raising flour
1 beaten egg yolk or 2 tablespoons milk, for glazing
1/4 cup sesame seeds

Cream together the butter, sugar and vanilla until smooth. Beat in the egg thoroughly, then add the milk. Stir in the flour and knead for a few seconds.

Take walnut-size pieces of dough and roll into long narrow strips, 4 in (10 cm) long and 1/2 in (1.25 cm) wide. Twist each strip into a circle, coil or any other shape desired. Brush lightly with the beaten egg yolk or milk and sprinkle with sesame seeds.

Place the biscuits on a well-greased baking tray and bake in a preheated moderate oven, 350°F (180°C/ Gas 4), until golden, about 20–25 minutes.

Shortbread biscuits Gh'raybeh

Makes 30 biscuits   **V**
Cooking time 25 minutes

1 lb (500 g) butter, preferably unsalted
1 cup caster sugar
7–8 cups plain flour, sifted
1/4 cup blanched almonds, for garnish

Cream the butter until it is white. Gradually beat in the sugar and continue beating for a further 5 minutes or until the mixture is smooth and creamy. Mix in the flour and knead by hand. The dough should be very soft, but if it is too soft for moulding, knead in a little more flour.

Mould the dough into small balls about the size of large walnuts. Press each ball down to make a flat bottom and place a blanched almond on top.

Place the biscuits on a baking tray (not too close together) and bake in a preheated 300–325°F (150–160°C) oven for 20–30 minutes. Be careful not to overcook or brown the biscuits—they should still be white when they come out of the oven or the taste will deteriorate.

Orange peel in syrup Mrubba ziffair

The orange peel for this recipe may be collected over a period and kept fresh by storing in the refrigerator in an airtight container.

V

6 large or 8 small thin-skinned oranges, for peel
2 cups sugar
2 cups water
1 tablespoon lemon juice

Scrape the surface of the oranges with a fork, then peel from the top to bottom with a sharp knife to make 6 segment strips. Scrape off some of the excess pith from the peel, then boil until soft, about 30 minutes. Drain well and soak in cold water for 24 hours, changing the water several times.

Roll up each strip and with a large needle, thread onto a heavy cotton thread, making a "necklace" to prevent the rolls from unravelling.

Bring the sugar and water to a boil, add the lemon juice and continue to boil for a further 5 minutes. Drop the "necklace" into the boiling syrup, turn down the heat and simmer gently, stirring occasionally with a wooden spoon, until the syrup thickens enough to thickly coat the back of the spoon.

Lift the necklace out of the syrup, remove the thread and drop the rolls into a jar. Allow the syrup to cool slightly, then pour over the rolls, making sure they are all covered. Seal with an airtight lid.

Serve rolls either with the syrup or rolled in sugar as crystallised fruit.

Fig jam Mrubba teen

If you cannot buy preroasted sesame seeds, you can roast your own by placing them on a hot, heavy-based frying pan and stirring until slightly browned.

Makes 3½ lb (1.75 kg)   V
Cooking time 50 minutes

2 lb (1 kg) fresh figs
1½ lb (750 g) sugar
1½ cups boiling water
1 tablespoon lemon juice
3/4 cup walnut pieces (optional)
1 tablespoon roasted sesame seeds
2 teaspoons ground aniseed (optional)
1/4 teaspoon powdered gum arabic (optional)

Wash the figs, then chop them and place in a large mixing bowl. Add the sugar, mix well and allow to stand for 3 hours or more.

Place the fig and sugar mixture in a large saucepan and simmer until juice appears, about 5 minutes. Turn heat to high and boil for 3 minutes. Add boiling water and lemon juice and boil steadily until the figs become very soft and tender and the water is absorbed, about 35 minutes. Add walnut pieces if using and sesame seeds and aniseed if using, and cook and stir for a further 5 minutes.

Remove from the heat and mix in the gum arabic if using. Cool slightly and pour into jars. Seal with airtight lids.

Variation Dried figs can be used instead of fresh figs, but they must be soaked overnight in enough water to just cover them—do not drain.

Pumpkin jam Tutlit ya'teen

Cooking time 35 minutes   V

1 pumpkin
sugar
water
1 tablespoon lemon juice
$^1/_2$ teaspoon powdered gum arabic (optional)
$^1/_2$ cup blanched slivered almonds

Peel and seed the pumpkin, then grate or grind the flesh and measure by cups. Measure 1 cup of sugar and $^1/_2$ cup of water for every 1 cup of pumpkin flesh. and place the sugar and water in a saucepan. Stir over a low heat until the sugar has dissolved. Bring to a boil, add lemon juice, turn down the heat to a simmer and stir constantly with a wooden spoon until the syrup is thick enough to thickly coat the back of the spoon.

Stir in the grated pumpkin flesh and, still stirring, continue to simmer until the mixture becomes soft and transparent. Add the gum arabic if using and cook for a further 3 minutes.

Remove from the heat and stir in the slivered almonds. Allow to cool slightly, then pour into jars. Seal with airtight lids.

Tahini and honey spread Tahini b'asel

V

Mix 2 parts tahini (see page 16) with 1 part honey for a sweet, nourishing spread.

Crystallised flowers Zah'rit succar

V

egg white
fruit blossom, violets, rose petals or mint leaves
caster sugar

Beat the egg white with a fork and pour it over the blossom, petals or leaves. Dip them into the caster sugar, then set aside on crinkled paper towels to dry in a cool place.

Use for garnishing puddings, cakes and other sweets.

beverages

In Lebanon the most popular drink is iced water! Other important nonalcoholic drinks are coffee, tea and sweet cordials, while favourite alcoholic beverages are arack, beer and wine.

A jug of iced water is always set on the table for each meal. At other times water is often drunk from a breah, which is a special water ewer with a spout. The breah is held above head level and water is poured directly into the mouth without the mouth touching the spout. It takes practice to master this method of drinking, but it is hygienic and certainly saves washing tumblers!

Coffee drinking is a ritual in Lebanon and visitors are always offered a cup as soon as they enter the house. Sugar is added to the coffee before it is brewed, so guests are asked whether they like it sweet, medium or without sugar. The coffee is served in very small cups, sometimes smaller than demitasse and often without handles. It is poured in the kitchen and presented on a tray, and the cups are handed around to each person. If guests do not want coffee they are offered tea or a cold cordial. Tea is always served weak and generally with slices of lemon. The traditional cordials are made from a thick fruit or fragrant syrup and diluted with water.

Alcoholic beverages are served with the mezza. The most popular of these is arack, a colourless but very potent anisated liquid which turns white as soon as water is added. Beers and wines of all types are imported into the country, but there are also many good local ones.

Red rosewater cordial Sharaab elwarid

Makes 4 cups syrup   V
Cooking time 15 minutes

few drops of red food colouring
4 cups Sugar syrup (see page 107)
iced water

Mix the food colouring with the sugar syrup, pour into a bottle with an airtight lid and store in the refrigerator. Dilute 2 tablespoons of syrup in a glass of iced water and serve as a cold cordial drink.

Mulberry syrup Sharaab el toot

Cooking time 20 minutes   V

mulberries
sugar

Place fresh, fully ripe black mulberries, together with a few red ones, in a muslin bag. Wearing rubber gloves, press the juice from the mulberries through the bag and into an earthenware or enamel container.

Measure the juice into an enamel or ceramic cooking pot and add 2 cups of sugar for every 1 cup of juice.

Boil the mixture vigorously, stirring with a wooden spoon until the syrup thickens. Remove from the heat, let cool until tepid and pour into bottles. Let stand until completely cool, then seal with airtight lids and store. When a bottle is unsealed for use, it should be kept in the refrigerator.

Use as a syrup on sweets or dilute 2 tablespoons in a glass of iced water to make a cold cordial drink.

Tamarind syrup Sharaab el tamarin

Tamarind pods can be purchased at Lebanese or Indian shops and some continental delicatessens.

Makes 3 cups syrup   V
Cooking time 15 minutes

1 lb (500 g) tamarind pods
3¹/₂ cups water
4 cups sugar

Clean and wash the tamarind pods. Place them in a large bowl, add the water and soak overnight. Drain the liquid into another bowl and reserve.

Extract the pulp from the pods by pressing them with a wooden spoon through a fine strainer.

Strain the extracted pulp back into the reserved liquid. Mix together, strain and squeeze through cheesecloth into a saucepan. Add the sugar.

Slowly bring the mixture to a boil, stirring constantly. Lower the heat and simmer until the syrup thickens. Remove from the heat, cool slightly and pour into bottles. Let stand until completely cool, seal with airtight lids.

Dilute 2 tablespoons of this syrup in a glass of iced water to make a cold cordial drink.

Variation To use this syrup for flavouring stews, stuffed vegetables and other foods, reduce the amount of sugar to 2 cups.

Lebanese coffee Ahweh

Lebanese coffee is traditionally made in a rakweh (see page 17), however a small saucepan with a pouring lip is a suitable substitute. Many people insist on roasting and grinding the beans just before making the coffee. If you do not want to do this, use the powdered Turkish coffee available at delicatessens and specialist food stores. Ordinary instant coffee is unsuitable.

V

For each demitasse cup of coffee, you will need:

1 demitasse cup of water
1–1¹/₂ level teaspoons sugar
1 heaped teaspoon powdered coffee (not instant)

Measure the water into a rakweh or small saucepan. Add the sugar and dissolve it by bringing the water to a boil and stirring. Remove from the heat, stir in the coffee, and very slowly bring to a boil again.

As soon as the coffee begins to rise, take it off the heat and allow to recede, then place it back on the heat to rise again. Repeat this procedure three times to extract maximum flavour from the coffee without overboiling it. Good Lebanese coffee will have a thick sediment in the bottom and a brown froth on top. This froth is called "ushta" (not to be confused with milk cream which is also called ushta).

Serve the coffee by pouring a little at a time into each cup so that the coffee, sediment and "ushta" are evenly distributed.

Alternative method Mix the coffee and sugar to a paste with a little of the water. Heat until it begins to bubble, add remainder of water and proceed as above.

index

equivalent terms

Most culinary terms in the English-speaking world can cross national borders without creating havoc in the kitchen. Nevertheless, local usage can produce some problems. The following list contains names of ingredients, equipment and cookery terms that are used in this book, but which may not be familiar to all readers.

Used in this book	Also known as
baking powder	double-acting baking powder
baking tray	baking sheet
bicarbonate of soda	baking soda
biscuits	cookies
boiler chicken	stewing chicken
pepper, red or green	sweet or bell pepper, capsicum
caster sugar	fine granulated sugar, superfine sugar
cornflour	cornstarch
desiccated coconut	shredded coconut
essence	extract
eggplant	aubergine
fillet (of meat)	tenderloin
frying pan	skillet
glacé (fruits)	candied
grill/griller	broil/broiler
hard-boiled egg	hard-cooked egg
icing sugar	confectioners' sugar
mincer	grinder
okra	gumbo, ladies' fingers
pastry	pie crust
pinch (of salt)	dash
plain flour	all-purpose flour
rosewater essence	rose extract
self-raising flour	self-rising flour
sieve	strain/strainer
(to) sift	(to) strain
spring onions	scallions, green onions
stone, seed, pip	pit
tea towel	dish towel, glass cloth
(to) whisk	(to) whip, beat
zucchini	courgettes

guide to weights and measures

The metric weights and metric fluid measures used in this book are those of Standards Australia. All cup and spoon measurements are level:

- The Australian Standard measuring cup has a capacity of 250 millilitres (250 ml).
- The Australian Standard tablespoon has a capacity of 20 millilitres (20 ml).

In all recipes metric equivalents of imperial measures are shown in parentheses e.g. 1 lb (500 g) beef. For successful cooking use either metric or imperial weights and measures—do not mix the two.

Weights

Imperial	Metric
1/3 oz	10 g
1/2 oz	15 g
3/4 oz	20 g
1 oz	30 g
2 oz	60 g
3 oz	90 g
4 oz (1/4 lb)	125 g
5 oz (1/3 lb)	150 g
6 oz	180 g
7 oz	220 g
8 oz (1/2 lb)	250 g
9 oz	280 g
10 oz	300 g
11 oz	330 g
12 oz (3/4 lb)	375 g
16 oz (1 lb)	500 g
2 lb	1 kg
3 lb	1.5 kg
4 lb	2 kg

Volume

Imperial	Metric	Cup
1 fl oz	30 ml	
2 fl oz	60 ml	1/4
3 fl oz	90 ml	1/3
4 fl oz	125 ml	1/2
5 fl oz	150 ml	2/3
6 fl oz	180 ml	3/4
8 fl oz	250 ml	1
10 fl oz	300 ml	1 1/4
12 fl oz	375 ml	1 1/2
13 fl oz	400 ml	1 2/3
14 fl oz	440 ml	1 3/4
16 fl oz	500 ml	2
24 fl oz	750 ml	3
32 fl oz	1L	4

Oven temperature guide

The Celsius (°C) and Fahrenheit (°F) temperatures in this chart apply to most electric ovens. Decrease by 25°F or 10°C for a gas oven or refer to the manufacturer's temperature guide. For temperatures below 325°F (160°C), do not decrease the given temperature.

Oven description	°C	°F	Gas Mark
Cool	110	225	1/4
	130	250	1/2
Very slow	140	275	1
	150	300	2
Slow	170	325	3
Moderate	180	350	4
	190	375	5
Moderately Hot	200	400	6
Fairly Hot	220	425	7
Hot	230	450	8
Very Hot	240	475	9
Extremely Hot	250	500	10

Useful conversions

1/4 teaspoon	1.25 ml
1/2 teaspoon	2.5 ml
1 teaspoon	5 ml
1 Australian tablespoon	20 ml (4 teaspoons)
1 UK/US tablespoon	15 ml (3 teaspoons)

Butter/Shortening

1 tablespoon	1/2 oz	15 g
1 1/2 tablespoons	3/4 oz	20 g
2 tablespoons	1 oz	30 g
3 tablespoons	1 1/2 oz	45 g